Listen to Spirit
KELVIN CRUICKSHANK

with Donna Fleming

PENGUIN BOOKS

PENGUIN

UK | USA | Canada | Ireland | Australia
India | New Zealand | South Africa | China

Penguin is an imprint of the Penguin Random House group of companies, whose addresses can be found at global.penguinrandomhouse.com.

First published by Penguin Random House New Zealand, 2020

1 3 5 7 9 10 8 6 4 2

Text © Kelvin Cruickshank, 2020
Images by Kelvin Cruickshank unless credited otherwise

The right of Donna Fleming to be identified as the author of this work in terms of section 96 of the Copyright Act 1994 is hereby asserted.

All rights reserved. Without limiting the rights under copyright reserved above, no part of this publication may be reproduced, stored in or introduced into a retrieval system, or transmitted, in any form or by any means (electronic, mechanical, photocopying, recording or otherwise), without the prior written permission of both the copyright owner and the above publisher of this book.

Design by Cat Taylor © Penguin Random House New Zealand
Cover photograph by Sarah Marshall
Background imagery by Ca Ku via Unsplash
Prepress by Image Centre Group
Printed and bound in Australia by Griffin Press, an Accredited ISO AS/NZS 14001 Environmental Management Systems Printer

A catalogue record for this book is available from the National Library of New Zealand.

ISBN 978-0-14-377444-0
eISBN 978-0-14377445-7

penguin.co.nz

Some names in this book have been changed to protect privacy.

Listen to Spirit

CONTENTS

SOUL-SEARCHING

1	A man named Curly	11
2	Worth a try	19
3	A visit from John	31
4	Missing people	43

OVERSEAS EXPERIENCE

5	*Voices from the Grave*	53
6	The director	65
7	The detective	75
8	TV, tears and taking a chance	85
9	The Land of the Rising Sun	99
10	Double act	109

BACK ON HOME SOIL

11	Time to pay it forward	125
12	Home, sweet home	137
13	Pain and payment	153
14	A warning from spirit	167
15	Random readings	179
16	Back to work	191
17	Dealing with sudden death	207
18	Lose the luggage	217
19	I can feel the love tonight	225
20	You've got a friend	239
21	Q and A	251
22	FAQ on KC	263
23	And on a final note	277

DEDICATION

Even for me, stopping to take a breath to relax can be rather hard at times, especially being so busy with the comings and goings of life. I have to remind myself to stop and LISTEN TO SPIRIT, too.

Our loved ones miss us just as much as we miss them every day, and they only want us to live a full and happy life.

When we forget to stop they will make us stop by sending us signs and creating events to remind us to slow down.

Don't forget they are often with us, sharing in our joys and sorrows, our hard times and fun times. They are proud of us.

I thank the spirit people for their consistent love and support, as I thank too my friends and family, as always.

Without each other we cannot continue to help in grave times of need.

We are blessed to be connected in life and death.

Always in heart,

KC

SOUL-SEARCHING

CHAPTER 1

A man named Curly

His name was Raymond Stirling, but to his family and friends he was known as 'Curly'. Although our paths had crossed when I was a child, I have only a very vague memory of him. He was a butcher, and I can recall when I was about four visiting his shop and the nice man in the stripy apron handing me one of those bright red sausages. I could never have known back then that Curly would one day change my life.

In January 2018 Curly, then 84, vanished from his Hamilton house. He'd just returned from spending a week on holiday at Cooks Beach, on the Coromandel Peninsula, with family members. A widower, and by all accounts a hell of a nice guy, Curly had mild dementia but was still living independently in his house.

When a support worker arrived to see Curly the day after he got home, there was no sign of him. The alarm was raised, and a search launched to find the much-loved father, grandfather and great-grandfather. He was quite frail, so the search team didn't think he could have gone too far. His house was fairly close to the Waikato River, so when he wasn't found after the first few days the fear was that he'd gone in the water. Boaties joined in the search but turned up nothing. Over a thousand people looked for Curly, from police and members of the Land Search and Rescue team, through to his family and friends, and local people who hadn't even known him.

The official search was suspended after the eleventh day, but the family refused to give up. His son Glenn devoted every moment he could to the search, including spending many hours on the Waikato in his kayak. But the searching turned up nothing.

Curly had vanished without a trace.

Looking for Curly

At the time, I had no idea any of this was happening. I was recovering from surgery on my back, which I'd seriously damaged when I fell off my boat, and so all of my energy was being channelled into getting better. Eventually, I was able to go back to work, and my first shows were in Hamilton, in the middle of February.

On the second night there, shortly before I was about to go on, my crew member Gemma came backstage and told me that the family of a missing man was in the audience. She knew that at that time I wasn't keen on dealing with missing persons cases because of the pressure they put me under. I found it hard because the desperation from the family was often so strong that it put me on edge and made it difficult for me to get the information I needed from spirit. I had also been involved in a few cases where, when

I'd got details from the person who was in spirit, the messages I had passed on were ignored and not followed up. There were times when I felt I wasn't trusted, which was really frustrating. As a result, I was going through a phase of wanting to avoid missing persons cases if I could.

That night I went out on stage and started the show, and, although I hadn't planned on saying anything, I found myself telling the audience: 'Look, I know there is a family here of someone who is missing, and I am sorry guys, but it is really hard for me to do these kind of cases, so I won't be able to help. Is the family here?'

A woman in the audience said, 'That's us.' It turned out to be Jo Stirling, Glenn's wife and Curly's daughter-in-law. And as soon as she spoke, Curly's spirit was there with me and it was all on. So I ignored my qualms, and did a reading for her. I couldn't help it: he was coming through loud and clear.

With Curly missing for four weeks by then the family had pretty much come to terms with the fact that he was dead, but it still must have been hard for Jo to hear me talking to him, because that confirmed he had definitely died.

And Curly was coming through really strongly, and making it clear that he wanted to be found so he could come home.

'You're supposed to help me,' he said to me.

He had his wife Margaret with him, and I started getting information that validated it really was them. There were some things that initially didn't make sense – for example, Curly showed me that he had been in the military, and Jo didn't know anything about that. But she checked later, and found out he had been in the territorials.

He showed me a beautifully made bed – in the style you learn in the army – and that really struck a chord with Jo. When Curly disappeared, his bed had been made like that, which was unusual. Margaret had always been the one who made the bed, and after she died Curly didn't make it neatly like she did – until the morning he vanished. The fact I knew the bed had been made so precisely was stunning. Other than the police, only the family knew that detail.

The reading with Jo was starting to take over the show and I needed to move on to other people, so I asked her if I could have a chat with her afterwards. We sat down for 15 minutes once I had finished signing books.

Curly had shown me what had happened to him, and it all made sense. What I saw was that he had gone to bed that night as usual, then woken up in the early hours of the morning. Because of his dementia, he'd become confused, and he thought he was a young man again. He got up and made his bed like he had when he was in the territorials, and then, because he didn't remember that Margaret had died, he decided to go in search of her. He left behind his glasses and his walking stick – he thought he was a young, healthy man who didn't need them – and toddled off looking for the love of his life, his beloved wife.

He walked quite a long distance, but he wasn't seen because it was the crack of dawn and there were bugger-all cars around. The further he went, the more disorientated and confused he got, and he ended up getting stressed. He crossed a road and went through paddocks and bush, looking for Margaret. He could see the lights of houses across a gully blinking at him, and he thought Margaret must be there, so he headed for them.

Sadly, poor Curly came to grief and fell down into a gully. And he showed me that that is where he had died, and where his body still lay.

Jo said to me, 'But the police think he went into the river.'

I shook my head. 'He is near water, a trickle of water, but not in the river.'

She gave me a look and said, 'Are you serious?'

'Completely serious. He's not in the river, love. There's no point looking there.' I was absolutely certain of that, because that's what

Curly was telling me: he was not in the water, but he was between two bridges. There were two possible areas where I thought he could be, and I hand-drew a couple of maps for Jo. 'This is where you should be looking,' I told her.

After I left the venue I couldn't stop thinking about Curly. The next morning I got up and drove to one of the areas where I had thought he could be, which was near the river. I said to him, 'You're not here, are you?'

He said, 'No, I am between two bridges but not these ones.'

I had to get home to the Bay of Islands, but I kept in touch with Jo, who had started looking in the other area I suggested. And although I was only too happy to help her however I could, the reality was I couldn't have just left it there, because Curly followed me home, and he wouldn't leave me alone.

That night, back in my own bed, I couldn't sleep because he was annoying me, in the nicest possible way. He talked to me the whole night, because he so desperately wanted to be found.

After tossing and turning for hours I got up, went straight to my office and sat down at my computer without even making my usual cup of coffee. I opened Google Maps, looked up Hamilton and, with Curly's spirit standing beside me, started searching for 'hot areas' where his body might be.

I got to one area of dense bush, which was located in the zone I had marked on the original map I had given Jo, and it felt like the right place. It was called Tauhara Park, and it was in the opposite direction to the river, where the search had been focused, and 2 kilometres from Curly's house. I was confident I was right, because Curly was going, 'That's it, that's it!' I took a screenshot of the map and then circled two adjoining areas on it. (Having said this, it did take me an hour to figure out how to draw on the map on the computer, as I'm not very savvy when it comes to that sort of stuff!) I then sent the map to Jo.

'This is where I think he is,' I wrote. 'Look in the top area first, if you can.'

I added, 'You'll probably need dogs – it's rough terrain.'

Jo went out with a friend who had dogs, and they covered a small part of the spot I'd marked out, but with no luck.

The next day was Saturday, and Jo and Glenn headed back to Tauhara Park with three friends. Searchers had been there at one stage, but they hadn't gone all the way down into the bush-clad gully.

A couple of hours after they headed off, I got a phone call from Jo. As soon as she said my name I could feel the emotion in her voice.

'KC,' she said, 'Glenn's found a body.'

Paying respects

Glenn found his dad beside a nearly empty creek at the bottom of a steep gully. When you looked at a map, his body was between two wooden bridge-like boardwalks.

Both Jo and I burst into tears when she called me, and afterwards I couldn't stop crying.

They were bittersweet tears – I was happy that the family had their beloved dad back, and knew what had happened to him, but I was also sad because they had lost someone they loved so much.

I had an overwhelming urge to give Jo and Glenn a big hug, so I jumped into my truck and drove down to Hamilton to see them the next day. I also needed to go to where Curly had been found so I could say a karakia (prayer) and pay my respects. Getting down to the site was tough-going for me because my back was still very painful, but it felt like the right thing to do.

Curly was with us, of course, and when I saw how far away we were from his home I said, 'Jeez, mate, how did you get all the way here?'

He replied: 'I was looking for my wife, son'.

Standing where he had died was very emotional and we were all feeling it. Then I started laughing.

'Glenn, your dad wants to know where his flowers are, you tight bugger.'

Those were Curly's words, not mine.

Glenn and Jo laughed. 'On the way to meet you we discussed getting some flowers to put on the site, but if we'd stopped to buy them we would have been late,' said Glenn.

That broke the ice, and helped lighten the atmosphere a little. Curly also mentioned his wallet.

'Is it missing? Are you still looking for it?' I asked Glenn.

'Yes, we are.'

Curly joked, 'Tell him there's no point, there's nothing in it!'

There was something else Curly said to me as we stood there. I passed it on to Glenn and Jo.

'Look, guys, it was really important for me to come here to say a karakia, but your dad has told me, "To tell the truth, I am not into all of that, so don't bother." '

Jo and Glenn cracked up again because they said that was exactly what Curly was like. No wonder he was saying, 'I'm home now, I'm with the missus and I'm happy, you don't need to go that far, young fella.' So I did as I was told and didn't say a prayer out loud, but I did do one quietly and quickly in my head. One of the things I gave thanks for was that Curly had trusted me to pass on his message. I was honoured he had done that. I was also thankful that Jo and Glenn were able to take Curly home and farewell him properly. Glenn would never have given up searching for his dad, and I honestly believe that if Curly hadn't been found, it would have broken his son.

CHAPTER 2

Worth a try

It's the nature of my job that I deal with a lot of death, tragedy and sadness. But one of the good things that comes out of it is that I get to meet some truly awesome people, like Jo and Glenn Stirling. They are two of the nicest people I have ever met, and I am beyond happy that I was able to find Curly for them.

> ### *Jo says*
>
> The more time passed without us finding Curly, the more desperate we were getting. We had tried everything, and

when my friend Gina suggested that we go to see a show Kelvin was doing in Hamilton I thought it was worth a try.

I had watched *Sensing Murder* and I knew a little bit about Kelvin. Although I have never been close-minded about mediums, I was one of those people who wasn't really sure about this kind of thing unless I'd had an experience of it myself.

Gina got in touch with Kelvin's staff member Gemma and told her what the situation was. Gemma said to come along to the show by all means, but there was no guarantee that Kelvin could help us.

When he came out on stage Kelvin was muttering to himself, saying, 'I am not doing this.' He acknowledged that Gemma had told him we were in the audience, and said he wouldn't be able to do anything.

Something was obviously troubling him, though, and then – bang – the floodgates opened. He asked where I was, and once I put my hand up he went into validation mode, giving us information like family names and mentioning a baby that was on the way.

After about three validations I knew he was onto something. I could feel a connection between us, and it seemed like everyone else in the audience disappeared, apart from Gina holding my hand. It felt like Kelvin was my hope.

He was firing away, as if he had verbal diarrhoea. He mentioned a couple of possible areas where he thought Curly could be.

He talked to me for ages and then went off to do something else, but he kept coming back to me. It was like something was bugging him. In the end he said, 'Rather than letting this hijack the show, I will talk to you afterwards.'

When Gina and I met up with him after the show, he drew us a couple of maps of the areas he had talked about. One of them included the site where we eventually found Curly, at Tauhara Park; the other was Cobham Drive.

The next morning Kelvin rang me to tell me he'd been up early and gone to the Cobham Drive area. 'I'm not getting any hits there,' he said. 'I'm in the wrong place, I think it is the other place; but I can't go there, I've got to get home.'

I could tell he wanted to keep helping but he had no option, he had to go.

I had written down everything I could remember about what Kelvin had said to me, and that day I went to Tauhara Park with Gina to start searching.

I noticed that things he had mentioned kept coming up. He'd talked about horses, and as we walked into the park there was a sign that said *Beware of the horses, please shut the gate.*

Every time I saw something like that I would get excited and think, We're onto it. But the park is such a big place and it did feel like we were looking for a needle in a haystack.

I sent Kelvin some photos of where we were searching, and he came back to me saying, 'No, go north.' He was so helpful; it was like we were working as a team and he was not going to let me down.

We didn't get anywhere that day, and because Kelvin had said that we would need to get dogs in because of the bush and the terrain, the next evening I got a friend with dogs to go with us.

At one stage we were by a gully and I had this unusual

feeling – I really wanted to go there, but it was so overgrown and I wasn't sure how to get in. I felt like I was on fire with adrenaline – people told me I was acting strangely. I couldn't help it.

We couldn't get in that time, and I felt despondent as we left the park that night. But as we drove away I spotted a way into that area and thought, Right, that's me tomorrow. It was Friday the next day, three days after the show, and when I went back to the park with a friend I got to where I felt I should be looking but didn't find anything. At one stage I was shouting, 'Where are you?' It was so frustrating because I somehow felt that I was close. It turned out that I was actually only 25 metres away from where Curly was.

That night I said to Glenn, 'We are going back there tomorrow. We have to keep looking there.'

It was tricky for Glenn. He wanted to support me in what I wanted to do, but he also felt a need to keep going back to the Waikato River to search, because that's where the police thought Curly had gone.

On the Saturday we managed to get a babysitter for our kids. Glenn went out on the river for four hours in the morning, and after lunch we and three friends set out from Curly's house. By then we had the Google map Kelvin had sent through, which helped to narrow things down. The area we were in had been searched by the Land Search and Rescue people. Interestingly, after Curly was found we saw the GPS maps showing where they had searched. When you looked at them, the markings looked like a rabbit warren, but there was one big gap – where the gully was.

The five of us worked our way methodically through the

long grass, staying 5 metres apart. Then we got to an area that for some reason felt to me like it was asking us to go in. I can't explain it.

One of the things Kelvin had said to me was: 'The moment someone says to you and Glenn that you are on the wrong track, you need to know that you are not, and you should stick with it.'

As we stood in this spot one of our friends said, 'This is ridiculous, there's no way Curly would have got all the way down here.' He was right, it did seem ridiculous because it was so far off the beaten track.

In that moment I looked over at Glenn and he said, 'Well, mate, if we don't go in here now I can guarantee that Jo and Gina will be back here tomorrow, and it's not safe. So let's keep going.'

Glenn went down into the gully, and for some reason I took a photo of him heading off. Within 10 minutes we heard him shouting, 'I've found a body!'

We rang the police straight away, and then I called Kelvin. I was in a bit of a state by that stage, but I was able to tell him, 'Thank you.'

It was a strange time, waiting there for the police to come. There was so much relief but also sadness. We thought, Finally, we have him home. It was not how we wanted him home, but we were able to lay him to rest.

I do think it is a miracle that we found Curly. From about day five after he went missing, the search was mostly focused on the river. There was still a lot of searching on land, but we expected that if that's where he was, he'd be just off a path. We thought he might have stumbled a little way or got tired and sat down, not that he would be a long way away down a gully.

It's strange; the day Curly was found it felt very natural to go into the area of bush where he was, it felt open to us. But the next day when we went back to show family the site, we walked straight past the place where we had entered. Even now, when we go to put flowers down there we have to really concentrate to find the entry point.

When Kelvin gave us those directions I just had to go with them, because, to be honest, at that stage they were all we had. We had chewed over every possible scenario we could think of. If Curly wasn't in the river, where was he? Had he got in a car with somebody maybe? We just didn't know, and we really were starting to think that we might never find him.

Glenn would never have got over it if we hadn't found Curly. He is such a driven man that he would never have rested. As well as desperately wanting to find my father-in-law, I really wanted to get back my husband and my kids' father.

At the start Glenn was not as open to getting help from a medium as I was, but I can tell you he's a huge Kelvin fan now. He thinks Kelvin's a legend. When people mention how Glenn found his dad, he says, 'No, I didn't. All I did was follow directions from my wife, who followed directions from Kelvin.'

If Kelvin hadn't given me that message at his show, Glenn would still be out on the river searching.

I know there are people who don't believe in the whole medium thing, but we can't deny what happened to us. It has absolutely changed my thinking, without a doubt. There are still a lot of unanswered things we don't understand, but we have peace because we found Curly. It could so easily have been a different outcome.

It was so nice for Kelvin to come and see us, and to go to the site. We have stayed in contact, and I feel like we have made a wonderful friend who we will be connected to for the rest of our lives. He was so good with our kids; he wasn't afraid to talk about their grandad. They are at peace with where their grandfather is now (with Nana), and I think a lot of that has to do with when Kelvin came to visit. They think he is amazing, and so do we.

Glenn and I have been going to some of his shows, including one not long after Curly was found. We were right at the back, and when Kelvin started doing a reading for a lady, her face came up on the video screen and we were surprised to see it was Glenn's auntie – Curly's sister. We had no idea she was there, and she didn't know we were there either.

Kelvin started talking to her about her sister-in-law, and Glenn said to me, 'That's my mum he's talking about.' Then he mentioned her brother, who had also passed away, but he had no idea that it was Curly.

Glenn and I were freaking out by this stage. We really lost it when Kelvin said to Glenn's auntie, 'I can see a boat with a blue tarpaulin on it. The boat is not being used and your brother says it should be.'

Glenn's auntie said, 'I don't have a boat, and I can't think of anyone with a boat.'

I said to Glenn, 'That's our boat. He's talking about the boat we just put the blue tarpaulin over. The kids keep asking when we are going to use it.'

The thing is, before it was ours, that boat belonged to Curly.

> In the end, Glenn couldn't stay quiet. He called out, 'I know about the boat.'
>
> Kelvin looked over and said, 'Hi, Glenn. What's this got to do with you?'
>
> When Glenn explained that the lady getting the reading was his auntie, Kelvin went, 'Oh my God, she's Curly's sister. I've got Curly with me!'
>
> It was an incredible moment.
>
> Kelvin changes so many people's lives, like he changed ours. I am still astonished by what he did for us, and I feel so blessed. It was a terribly tragic situation, but it was also a miracle. We are so grateful, and we feel it is so important to acknowledge what he did. We are not afraid to let people know what Kelvin can do, because one day hopefully he will be asked for his help and it will be in time to find someone alive. He is a very special man.

This is my purpose

For me, finding Curly was a life-changing experience, because it was the first time that – as far as I am aware – a medium in New Zealand was able to locate the body of a missing person. In some ways it offered concrete validation of what I do. That was important because while a lot of people are open to the idea that it is possible to talk to those who have passed away, there are plenty of others who aren't. This means that at times I have been accused of everything from being unhinged and deluded, through to being a charlatan and a scammer. Mediums like me have been described as 'grief vampires', and told we prey on the vulnerable. Yet everything I do, I do to help others.

WORTH A TRY

I didn't ask to have this ability; it was something I was born with. It took me a long time to come to terms with, and it nearly broke me in the process. Being able to see dead people has caused me huge pain, and it made me feel like a misfit when I was younger, until I realised that I was given this gift for a reason. I have to use my abilities to connect spirit with their loved ones that are still on this side of life; it's what I am here to do.

Doing that helps to bring peace of mind to those who are grieving, because I can tell them their family members, partners or friends are okay. I can pass on important messages and hopefully help to ease some of the crippling pain that comes with grief. I can let them know that their loved ones may no longer be here physically, but their souls live on, and they are never far away.

With the knowledge I have gained over the years, I can also reassure people about death, and help them to understand what happens when you die.

And being able to communicate with spirit also means that in some cases I can find out what happened to people who have disappeared or been murdered. Sometimes, spirit is able to tell me how they died or who was responsible. They can also tell me where they are. Like Curly did.

Despite all the criticism I get, I've seen how I've been able to help many, many people in the 20-plus years I have been doing this. That's what matters.

It is rewarding to be able to pass on messages from a mother to her children to let them know she no longer has crippling arthritis in her hands and can knit once more, and she's so, so grateful to the children for looking after her the way they did at the end. Or to be able to tell the parents of a child who died in an accident that it was not their fault, and their little one is safe and well on the other side, being looked after by their nan.

But to be able to locate missing people and give their families closure, or to uncover the truth about how someone died . . . I really feel like this is my purpose. It's something I would love to be able to focus on more, because it would bring peace to so many people who can't get on with their lives because they don't know what fate befell someone they love.

I am convinced that if I am meant to help, I will be able to. And I'm hoping there will be many more people out there like Jo and Glenn, who are able to find a missing loved one because they trust me, and because that person in spirit also trusts me enough to tell me where they are.

Proud of what I do

After I found Curly I told only a handful of people what had happened. Although it was a huge deal, I didn't want to go shouting about it from the rooftops. It wasn't about me.

However, Jo and Glenn did talk about the part I had played, including thanking me at Curly's funeral. And when the media found out I'd been involved, there were a couple of stories in newspapers, a magazine and online about what had happened. Even so, mention of my part in finding Curly was pretty minimal, which I was okay with. Nevertheless, there was some negative feedback that I'd talked publicly about being involved, which was upsetting.

There have been plenty of times when the work I have done has stayed under the radar for very good reasons, and, apart from me and a handful of people involved, nobody will ever know what happened. And rightly so.

But helping to bring Curly home was the best thing I've ever done in my career as a medium. I am proud of what I do, and I was honoured that in this case I could help, and save his loved ones from further heartache and distress. Jo and Glenn were grateful, and that's what matters. I brushed aside the negativity and told myself, 'KC, this might be the only time you can find a missing person like this, just be glad it happened.'

And then, nearly a year to the day after Curly was found, it happened again.

CHAPTER 3

A visit from John

I'd gone to bed one Thursday night in February 2019 but hadn't yet dropped off to sleep when the spirit of a Māori elder suddenly appeared at the end of my bed.

'Kia ora, matua. What's going on here?' I enquired, then went into what I call being 'in the zone', which is a sort of trance, where I'm not asleep but not fully awake either. This lovely old guy proceeded to show me a location with trees and skid sites – areas in a forest where the trees have been felled and stacked up. I saw a steep gully, and the man lying in it. I could see the position his body was in so clearly that a couple of days later I got a friend to take a photo of me lying just like him.

The guy showed me a bandage on his leg, which I took to mean that he had a problem with it. He also indicated that his wife had passed over before him.

I saw everything very clearly, but had no idea why I was being shown these things.

What I didn't know then was that a 77-year-old man named John Mohi had gone missing in the small Bay of Plenty town of Maketu. Like Raymond Stirling, John had mild dementia. He used to go for a walk for a couple of hours every day, but one Monday he didn't come home. His disappearance was completely out of character and his family were immediately very worried. A search was launched but failed to find him.

A couple of days after the Māori elder visited me, I got up on the Saturday morning, made a coffee and was checking my emails when I saw one from a member of John's family asking for help. It was very respectful and humble, and included a phone number, so without really thinking about it I picked up the phone and called the sender, a woman named Rubeena.

I got the feeling that the guy who'd come to see me was the missing man, but I needed to confirm that, so I asked her a few questions. Yes, he did have something wrong with his leg, and yes, his wife had died, she told me.

John was there with me in spirit, and he said there was a female family member I was meant to speak to, but it was not Rubeena.

'I need to talk to the person who is closest to the investigation,' I said.

'That will be Ronnie,' said Rubeena. One of John's granddaughters, Ronnie, had been the one working closest with the police, and doing the media interviews.

'Can you get her to call me, please? She's the one I need to talk to.'

Ronnie phoned me 20 minutes later, but she didn't appear to know who I was.

A VISIT FROM JOHN

'I know you don't know me,' I told her, 'but I need to tell you that your koro came to me in a vision the other night and there are some things I have to tell you. Don't try to analyse everything and figure out how I know this, just trust me.'

She seemed prepared to listen, so I started talking.

I mentioned that John had gone off in search of his late wife – just like Curly had – and I said she'd had heart problems, because he was showing me her heart. Then I told her about the stand of trees with the cleared skid sites. 'There are two of these sites, and if you draw a line between them he's smack-bang in the middle, down a steep gully.'

'I know where that is,' Ronnie said. And I could tell by her voice that her heart was racing.

'Then go,' I told her.

'I'm gone,' she said.

The entire conversation lasted only eight minutes, but it was enough to convince Ronnie to act straight away. She immediately went to the hall where the search and rescue team was based and told them I had given her a location where I thought her koro (grandfather) was. (By then she had realised who I was.)

Apparently everyone stopped what they were doing and paid attention, and then the searchers went to the area I had pinpointed. The interesting thing was that while I had been right about there being two skid sites, one of them was so recent that a lot of people hadn't realised it was there. It certainly wasn't on Google Maps – I couldn't have seen it by looking online.

The search and rescue team followed my instructions, drawing a line between the two skid sites and then heading for the middle. A cadaver dog – one that is trained to pick up the scent of dead bodies – went down the very steep gully, and that's where John's body was found. He was lying in the grass, in the position I had described. As it turned out, it was a position he liked to sleep in. Later, when I showed Ronnie the photo of me in that position, she said, 'Oh my God, that's how Koro sleeps.'

A very special whānau

It was about 7.30 p.m. that evening when Rubeena phoned me back. She could barely speak because she was crying so much, but she managed to tell me that John had been found.

'Thank you,' she said. 'Thank you, Kelvin.'

I was crying, too. 'I'm so sorry for your loss, but I am pleased you have got him home,' I told her.

Just as when Curly was found, I was overwhelmed, shocked and very emotional. I was so glad I could help and that they didn't have to spend weeks – or even longer – in that horrible limbo of not knowing what had happened. I was thankful to John for coming to me, and trusting me to help his mokopuna find him.

What I believe happened, because John showed me, was that during his walk that day his dementia started to kick in. He got confused and went off in search of his late wife, Waimeha. He cut through a paddock and went up a hill. By the time he got to the top he was puffed, hot (it was a tropical 32 degrees Celsius that day) and dehydrated. He went over a broken fence, and then fell into a very steep bush-covered ravine. John showed me that he survived the fall and tried to get up and walk away, but couldn't. So he lay down in the grass, in the position he liked to sleep in, and that's where he passed.

I found out later that searchers had been in the area, but they hadn't gone down to the bottom of the ravine. My understanding is that the search was moving away from that particular place to focus on another area, and that it may not have been searched again. John might never have been found.

A VISIT FROM JOHN

But the man who had come to me in spirit desperately wanted his body to be recovered. His family meant the world to him, and he could see how much they were hurting. He was a very powerful man, the sort of person who was well respected, but he was also very humble. He asked for my help, and I was so glad I was able to give it to him.

As soon as I heard his body had been located, I had an overwhelming urge to drive down to Maketu to see Ronnie, Rubeena and the rest of John's whānau. There needed to be an exchange of energy between me and the family so I could close down after everything that had happened. I also needed to hug them, and to see the site where John was found. I would have gone straight away if it wasn't for a couple of friends who were at my house at the time. They told me not to be stupid: it was a six-hour drive, and if I left then and there, like I wanted to, I'd arrive in the Bay of Plenty at 2 a.m. So instead I got up at 6 a.m. and a friend and I drove down. As soon as we got over the Kaimai Ranges and into the Bay of Plenty, John was in the back seat, telling me things about himself and his family.

'Sorry, matua, but do you think you can wait until we get to Maketu, and then I can pass this information on to everyone as you tell me?' I asked. 'That way it will be fresh.'

'Of course,' he said. 'There's just one thing: can I bring my beautiful wife with me?'

I could feel how happy he was to have been reunited with her.

'Of course you can,' I said.

That afternoon in Maketu with John Mohi's whanau is one of the most incredible experiences I have ever had. Dozens of family members were waiting for me in the community hall, and I have never felt so much love from a room full of strangers in my whole life. After a welcome involving speeches and waiata (song) I got to meet and hug everyone, and I'd never been hugged like that in my life. I could feel the love and the gratitude. It was just beautiful, absolutely outstanding.

When I gave my speech I tried to be professional, but the tears started pouring down my face and I could barely keep it together. I thanked everyone for trusting me, and then I told them that their koro was there with me.

'Are you okay if I tell you a few things?' I asked them. They were all good with that, so I was able to pass on some messages, including the fact that John was there with his wife. He also asked me to tell Ronnie that he knew she would never, ever have given up on finding him, which was why he'd told me to talk to her.

There was something else John wanted me to tell everyone.

'He says he was the kind of person raised with the Bible, and because of that he didn't believe in people like me, who see spirit. He wants you to know that he understands now how it works and he is at peace with it.'

Afterwards Ronnie's husband, Justin, took me to the site where John had been found. We did a karakia and sung some waiata, paying our respects to him. I laid some yellow wildflowers, and once again I thanked him for trusting me.

I can only help if wairua (spirit) come to me. I can't force anything, and nor can the family of the missing person. John's whānau were so respectful towards me, there was no pressure, even though they were so desperate to find him. They really are amazing people, and being able to help them was a huge honour for me.

Ronnie says

When Rubeena got me to speak to Kelvin on the phone, it didn't click who he was. I wasn't really into all of that stuff, to be honest. Over the week of the search I had been contacted by a few psychics and some of them had sent me on wild goose chases. I wasn't happy about that, and so I didn't really want to talk to anyone else.

But when Rubeena rang and asked me to speak to Kelvin, I was running out of options. I was at the stage where I would take anything I got — I just wanted to find my grandfather. I thought, If Rubeena trusts this person, I will give it a go.

I don't know what it was, but as soon as he started talking to me, something felt different. He said he needed to know if he had the right person, and asked me about my grandfather, including if he had something wrong with his left leg or hip. He did; it was an old injury. He also asked if my nan had died before my grandfather, and mentioned a scar on her heart. She'd had a triple bypass.

He talked about someone who had passed from cancer, and it wasn't until later I thought about my best friend. She'd died from cancer, and in fact I'd messaged her old Facebook account and said, 'Hey, mate, if you have some time today, can you please help me find my grandad?'

Kelvin told me he didn't know Maketu at all, but when he started talking about my grandfather going through a paddock and up a hill, and described areas where trees had been felled, I knew exactly where he meant. It had been searched, but the gully was very difficult to get down because it was so steep.

We weren't on the phone for all that long, and when I got off I told my family I'd had some information from a guy called Kelvin. When they said 'He's the fella off *Sensing Murder*', I said 'No, I don't think so.' Then I realised that — wow — it *was* him. I trusted what he said, and I knew in my heart that my grandfather would be found.

I went straight to the ops team who were organising the search and pointed out the area Kelvin had told me about.

'We need to get a team in there now,' I said.

They asked why, and my sister-in-law, who was with me, said, 'Because Kelvin Cruickshank told her to go there.'

They said 'You mean the psychic?', and I told them 'I know you aren't into this sort of thing, but I know in my heart that he is right, and I want the team to go there now.'

Luckily there are some open-minded police officers there, and they said, 'Whatever you feel you want to do, we will do it.'

They took the cadaver dogs with them. It was not long afterwards that I got a phone call to tell me that a police officer was coming to see me. He broke the news that my grandfather had been found. With the information from Kelvin, it had taken them just 20 minutes to locate him. Twenty minutes.

Of course my family had been hoping for the best, but we were also realistic, and by the time he'd been missing for four days we knew that he was probably gone and we were looking for a body. It was still hard, though, to hear that he had passed, but we were just relieved his body had been found. It could have been weeks before we found him, or we might not have found him at all.

It was so good of Kelvin to come down to Maketu the next day; he didn't have to do that. It was very emotional when we got to say thank you to him.

He was very down-to-earth, just a normal guy, but it can't be easy having the gift that he has. I really feel for him because he has to deal with sad things all the time.

It was interesting when he said that he felt I was the one he had to speak to. My grandfather was all about his grandkids, he did so much for us all, but I was the one who would go around and growl at him: 'Have you taken your medication? Have you been to the doctor?' He'd see me coming and go, 'Oh, here we go again.'

Kelvin said he had to talk to me because I was the strongest, and it is true — I am the wahine toa of the family.

It was also interesting to hear about my grandfather going to Kelvin's house. That was the sort of thing he would have done: he wouldn't have left Kelvin alone until he did what he wanted him to do.

After the news came out that my grandfather had been found, I told one journalist, who had been very respectful to me all week, about Kelvin being involved. I felt that people needed to know what he did, and give him some recognition.

We found my grandfather because of Kelvin. Getting my grandfather back gave us peace of mind and made the grieving easier. It also meant we could start the healing process. It would have been terrible to have been left not knowing what had happened to him and to not be able to say goodbye.

Thanks to Kelvin, we do know, and we are all very grateful.

A helping hand

There were a few stories in newspapers and a magazine about how I had helped to find John Mohi, but, just as with Curly, most media outlets didn't seem interested in what I had done. While they had always been quick to have a go at me in the past when the information I gave on *Sensing Murder* came to nothing (usually because nobody acted on it), it seemed finding two missing people in the space of a year wasn't worthy of coverage.

Again, this is annoying, if only because it represents a missed opportunity to show that the ability to talk to dead people is real, and can make a difference. To show that there is another possible avenue of action for people in distress.

I believe I can help, if I am meant to.

And I strongly believe that in the case of John I was meant to find him. When I got off the phone to Ronnie on that Saturday, after describing where her grandfather was, I sat on my deck with my friend Matua Tata, who was staying with me, and repeated the conversation to him. Everyone calls Matua Tata 'Uncle', and if you've read some of my other books you will know what an amazing person he is.

Uncle is very spiritually gifted, and he has been a great mentor to me throughout my life. I value his advice very much, and I am in awe of how wise he is. When I had finished telling him about what I'd said to Ronnie, he turned to me.

'They will find John Mohi today,' he predicted. 'He'll go home.'

He was right, as it turned out. And I believe he was also right about something else he said to me later that night, after we heard that John had been found.

'You know, don't you, Kelvin, that Curly brought John to you? He's the reason John was found.'

I believe Uncle's right. I believe that the reason John Mohi turned up in my bedroom that night, asking for help, was because Curly pointed him in my direction.

You can say I'm mad as much as you like, but spirit really do work in amazing ways. John and Curly did not know each other on this side of life, but the parallels between their cases are incredible. Both had mild dementia, both walked off looking for their late wives, both fell down steep gullies into thick bush where they might never have been discovered.

Thanks to Jo Stirling coming to my show a year earlier and asking for help to find her father-in-law, I developed a connection to Curly. And I believe that this lovely old guy, when he saw someone else in spirit whose family was desperate to find him, nudged John in my direction so I could help him, too.

I just hope he does more of that. I really want to help as many Curlys and Johns, and their families, as I possibly can.

CHAPTER 4

Missing people

According to New Zealand Police, there are currently more than 350 people in this country who have been missing for more than a year. You read that right – 350. That means hundreds of family members and friends have been left with a huge gap in their lives, and with the anguish of not knowing where their loved ones are and what has happened to them.

To all those parents reading this: have you ever been in a shop or a mall when your child disappears on you, and when you can't find them straight away you get that horrible churning feeling deep down in the pit of your stomach? Or can you remember what it felt like when you were a kid and you thought your mum had gone ahead to the frozen-food aisle in the supermarket while you stayed behind, eyeing up the lollies, only to be unable to spot her when you managed to drag yourself away from the jelly beans and Jaffas? Remember that sickening feeling of panic, not knowing where she was?

Imagine what it must be like, then, for the families of all those people who actually go missing, and are not just out of sight for a few minutes. How it must feel for the Jos and Glenns and Ronnies of this world whose loved one is there one minute and gone the next. John Mohi's whānau had to wait an agonising five days to find out what had happened to him; for the Stirlings it was a month.

But what about those people who spend years – and in some cases the rest of their lives – having no idea where their parent or child or partner or friend is? They have to navigate their way through each and every day with an ache deep inside them because this person has gone, and they don't know what happened. How hideous must that be?

Missing persons readings really tear me up, and I wish I had been able to get the same results for all of the families I have read for over the years that I did for the Stirling and the Mohi families.

There are a few reasons why I think that hasn't happened. One is that I can only go on what spirit tells me, and sometimes the messages I get don't make sense. Or I am deliberately given misleading information by spirit who don't want to be found. That's happened before.

But what it often comes down to is whether or not people are prepared to trust me. Jo trusted me, so did Ronnie. In Curly's case, it seemed hard to believe that a frail elderly man could have walked 2 kilometres from his home. But Jo didn't question that I said he was so far away, and she followed through on it. Ronnie didn't analyse where the information I gave her came from, she took it and went straight to the search team with it.

But unfortunately I don't always get that response. In some cases it's because what I say doesn't fit in with other people's theories, so they dismiss it. Other times it's because they simply don't believe I am communicating with dead people and won't even make the effort to look into what I have said. Fair enough, I guess, that's their decision. But it can be frustrating and often upsetting for me.

One case I tried to help with, after I was approached by friends of the person who had gone missing, went nowhere despite the person coming to me in spirit and passing on some information. Unfortunately the family doesn't want to know, despite the success I've had with Curly and John. That's their right, but what harm would it have done to follow up on what I was seeing?

I also wish the police would be more open-minded when it comes to the information that mediums can give them. I know there are some officers out there who will take the chance, like the police working on the search operation for John Mohi, who listened to Ronnie when she turned up at the search HQ after her phone conversation with me.

I know police searches can be expensive and take up a lot of resources, and that the last thing they want to do is be led on a wild goose chase by someone whose information comes from a dead person. But what if it is not a wild goose chase? What if I do have relevant information because it has come directly from the person at the heart of the case? Isn't it worth looking into?

A family's pain

Along with the John Mohi and Raymond Stirling cases, there was another missing persons one that I was involved with a while back where a body was eventually recovered. But the part I played won't be made public. I can't go into detail about why that is or what happened – it's complicated. But what I can say is that it is one of the most traumatic cases I have been involved in.

The relatives approached my team about a family member who had gone missing, and gave them a number for me to call. When I phoned the number and spoke to them the spirit of this missing person immediately came through, which, sadly, meant they had died. Getting information out of this person in spirit proved to be difficult because there were certain things about their life that they didn't want their family or me to know about. So I had to handle things very delicately to try to win them over.

Just as it can take a while to get a stranger to open up to you in this side of life, it can take some time to win spirit's trust. You have to give them a bit of time to warm to you, which I did. I also had to calm this spirit down because they were distressed about what had happened to them. And when they showed me what that was, I understood why. Their death was brutal.

I did not want to tell the family what I had seen, but they insisted they needed to know. I tried to explain it as gently as I could, but one family member let out a scream that chilled me to the core. It took me back to when I was seven, and living in the small Waikato community of Rotongaro. My Auntie Nola – who was not a relative, but a neighbour everyone called auntie – was stabbed to death by a local teenage boy. When my mum was told the news she screamed, and I have never been able to forget that sound. Hearing something so similar again from the family of this person just about snapped me in two.

I could feel the family's terrible pain, and I became fixated on helping them to bring their loved one home. A member of my team also shared my deep concern, and together the two of us spent many hours going through the jumble of information spirit had given me, trying to work out where this person was.

My team member was so determined to help the family she wanted to drive around an area I'd pinpointed, looking for possible landmarks spirit had shown me. I had to say to her, 'No way. Don't even think about it – do you know how dangerous that could be?' This was a very serious situation; you don't muck around with that sort of stuff. Thankfully, she listened to me and didn't go.

Eventually a body was found, and the circumstances surrounding the death matched what I had told the family. I can't tell you what led to the discovery, other than that information I was able to give the family set off a chain of events that meant they got their precious one back. The relief I felt was huge.

This case has had a massive impact on me, and while it has been utterly heart-wrenching, it is one more experience that has shown me that if I am given the opportunity to help and am trusted, I just may be able to make a difference.

Out of the blue

Normally I become involved in missing persons cases only if I am asked to help. If the family approaches me, like Jo Stirling did, I will see what I can do. When John Mohi turned up in my house, I didn't go to Google to see if I could figure out who this Māori elder might be. I knew if I was meant to be involved in whatever was going on with him, the family would come to me. And they did.

On the very rare occasions that I watch the TV news and there's an item about a missing person, a scenario of what has happened to them might pop into my head. For example, years ago I saw something on the news about a missing person and got an image of a barrel in my mind. I instantly knew that's where their body was, jammed inside a barrel.

People often ask if I can tell them what happened in high-profile cases, like the disappearance of Madeleine McCann. I may have my theories, but unless the family comes to me and specifically asks for my help, then I am not going to start asking spirit for answers and sharing that information around.

However, like just about everything in my life, there are exceptions to the rule. Sometimes spirit come to me without the family being involved because they desperately want to be found. There might be a very tenuous link that connects us, but they come through anyway.

This happened one afternoon when a friend and I were discussing missing persons cases and how devastating it must be for a parent not to know where their child is. My mate mentioned that she had once had a brief encounter with a woman whose adult son had gone missing and never been found. 'I don't know how she carries on with day-to-day life, just not knowing,' my friend said. 'It would break me.'

All of a sudden, as she spoke, the spirit of this guy appeared in my living room, standing next to my TV. It was unusual that he would show up, because he had no connection to my friend – she had never met him, and had only met his mum once. But he came through loud and clear.

And not only did he show up, but he showed me what had happened to him, and it wasn't nice. My friend said that to her knowledge the theory was that he had probably either died accidentally or committed suicide. But what he was showing me was that he had been murdered.

It was like having a movie screening in my mind – I could see the circumstances leading up to his death, I could see how he was killed, and I could see the person who did it. I was shown how they crossed paths, and I could even see the type of vehicle this person drove, including the colour of some of the paintwork on it, and what they did for a living. I was also given a couple of names.

I was shown where the body was buried, along with nearby landmarks. The whole experience was freaky, especially as it had come completely out of the blue.

So now what? What are you supposed to do when something like that happens? I don't know the mother and, although my friend could probably track her down, I would have to be very careful about how I approach her. I can't just get in touch out of the blue and say: 'Hey, I'm that guy off the TV who talks to dead people, and your son has just told me he was brutally murdered.'

I don't know if the mum is open to spirit and mediums, and, even if she is, what I have to tell her is going to be devastating.

But her boy came to me for a reason, and if I am meant to help his family learn what happened to him, then I will. The information his spirit has passed on to me might just lead to his body being found, which in turn could provide clues as to who the killer is. It just might require a bit more mahi (work) on my part and some sensitive handling.

In the meantime, the next time I am in the area where he showed me his body might be, I'm going to drive around and check out the landmarks. I'm pretty sure they are going to match what he showed me that day.

It would be so good if he can be found, and if his family can have some closure. And hopefully that person out there who has so far got away with his killing will be brought to justice.

Not meant to be

So, having just told you all about the times when I have been able to help find missing people, I now need to talk about those times when I can't do anything. I may desperately want to help, but I have had to come to terms with the fact that sometimes there is nothing I can do, and not just because nobody will follow through on the messages I get.

This was brought home to me a few years back when a woman who lived not too far from me went missing. The family got in touch and asked if I could please help. I said I was happy to, but it would depend on if spirit came through to me.

'If I get anything, I will let you know straight away, but please don't be upset if you don't hear from me – it won't be that I've forgotten, but that I've got nothing,' I told them.

In this case, that was precisely what happened. Her spirit never came to me. Whenever I drove past the area she was from to go fishing, I would say a karakia in case she wanted to make contact. Unlike other spirit, though, who have actually hopped into my car next to me when I've been driving past a place of significance, she did not hitch a ride. She didn't do a John Mohi and show up at my house either. There was absolutely nothing.

Her body was eventually found, I am pleased to say, and her family are no longer stuck in that horrible limbo of not knowing where she is. In fact, she was found in the area I regularly drove past, so you would have thought her spirit might have seen that as an opportunity to use me and my abilities. The fact is, it just wasn't meant to be, for whatever reason.

OVERSEAS EXPERIENCE

CHAPTER 5

Voices from the Grave

It's not every day you end up with the spirit of an infamous serial killer sitting in the front passenger seat of your car alongside you. Thankfully. But that was the situation I found myself in after returning home following a stint working in the United States.

I'd had an encounter with the spirit of this particular low-life while working on a TV show there. I can't tell you his name, because the programme hasn't aired yet, but most of you would recognise it. He was an evil, evil man, and what he did was just hideous. I didn't expect him to follow me back to New Zealand, though, so it was a shock when he turned up in my car, trying to communicate with me. I have put up a kind of spiritual safety-dome over my home to keep dark stuff out, and the moment I turned into my driveway he was gone. I know he can't hurt me because I have protection in place, but still, it was a relief when he went.

That was just one example of the many bizarre, weird, freaky and downright scary things that have happened to me since I became involved with this TV programme four years ago. Don't get me wrong, I absolutely love working on the show – it's fascinating, thrilling and exciting. It has had a huge impact on my life, and I'm ready for the challenges that come with doing it. But some of the experiences I have had are mind-blowing, even for me, and that's putting it politely.

Unfortunately, at the moment I can't share many details about what I have been doing, because everything is being kept under wraps until the series screens. But I can reveal a little of what I have been up to without giving away too much, to give you an idea of the situations I have ended up in.

The doctor's house

It was back in mid-2016 that I first started working as one of three mediums on a TV show which was then titled *Haunted Hollywood*. (You may recall a chapter about it in my previous book *Surrounded by Spirit*.) I'd been contacted by an American TV producer and director called Alisa Statman – otherwise known as Lisa – who found me after seeing episodes of *Sensing Murder* on YouTube. After a Skype interview, in which I read for her and was able to pass on messages from her partner who had died of cancer, she asked if I could come to Los Angeles to film an episode at a house in a posh part of town.

The three-storey, 1920s Spanish-style mansion was the site of a horrific murder-suicide committed by a well-respected Hollywood doctor. After killing his wife, he had attempted to kill one of their three children, then took a drug overdose, lay down on his bed, and died.

After that dreadful night, the children moved out, and the house was sold 'as is' to a couple in the early 1960s. It remained full of the doctor's family's furniture to appear as if someone was living there, but the new owners never moved in.

In 2016 Lisa got the opportunity to film an episode of her show there. She arranged for me and Joe Perreta, another medium she'd hired, to visit the property, along with a regular camera crew and what I call the ghost-busting team – the people using special spooky cameras and audio equipment that pick up spirit energy. More about them later.

I encountered several spirits as soon as I arrived at the house, including the doctor and his murdered wife. There was also a gorgeous blonde chick, who was looking out the window when I arrived, and hung around for a while. I didn't know who she was, or how she fitted in to the house, but I could tell she was one of the good guys, and she was just kind of observing.

The doctor's wife, on the other hand, showed me what had happened to her, giving me images of medical instruments and a doctor's bag. I was able to explain to her that I had cleared away negative energy by saying a karakia, or prayer, and that it was safe for her to cross over to the other side.

Family in spirit then appeared to take her home, which was lovely, and very emotional for me. Unfortunately, the spirit of her husband was there, too, and dealing with him wasn't quite so peaceful. He was flipping out at me, screaming at me to get out of his house.

'Dude, calm down,' I told him once I had helped his wife to cross over. 'I'm out of here.'

I went downstairs, but I didn't actually leave the house. As I walked through the decaying rooms I was seeing a whole load of images in my mind, and I was pretty sure they weren't connected to the murder of the doctor's wife. Other stuff had happened in that house in the years it had stood empty, and it wasn't good.

Things really kicked off when I got down to the basement. Instantly I knew that the doctor's wife was not the only person to have been murdered in the house, because with me was the spirit of a young woman who had been raped and murdered. I got the feeling she was Mexican or South American, and that her death had something to do with the drug trade.

I also realised that the basement contained two portals. I don't usually talk about these sorts of things, because it's a pretty heavy subject and it freaks people out – to be honest, it freaks me out. But basically portals are entry points set up by people dabbling in evil stuff so that dark energy can come and go. In layman's terms, they are tunnels to the underworld. People had been holding séances in the house – that was one of the images I had seen when I was upstairs – and had attracted some very negative spirit.

I surrounded myself in white light and said a karakia, then I shut down one of the portals to keep out the negativity. As I did I could see that a group of spirit people were trapped there, so I called them through into the light. These were not dark spirits, but people who had endured unspeakable things, and they had been held there for a very long time. They were finally able to go home.

I continued to pray, asking for the room to be cleansed of the bad stuff, and then I hightailed it outside to try to calm down and get my breath back. It had all been very scary and draining.

However, that was not the end of it, because I felt the need to go back in and check out the crawl space between the house and the ground. While I was down there the spirit of the girl who had been raped and murdered was with me, and at one stage she grabbed my leg and held onto it. The whole time this was happening, the spirit-sensing cameras were going berserk.

While I was in the crawl space I found some bits of bone. We don't know if they are tied into the scary stuff that has happened in the house over the decades it has sat there abandoned. They are being investigated further.

But what I do know is that by going down into the basement and the crawl space, and finding the portals, I had got a hell of a lot more than anyone bargained for, and opened a whole can of worms.

An encounter with pure evil

When Lisa decided to film in the house she had no idea whatsoever that it contained the portals, which connected it to some evil stuff that has been going on in Los Angeles for many years, and is still happening. I can't go into great detail, but what I can say is that we're not talking about ordinary (for want of a better word) murders. This involves secret societies and satanic worship. We're talking about a group of people who believe they have to take lives in this life so they can have slaves in the afterlife. Because of what has been done to these victims, they are unable to cross over into the light, and they become trapped. It is very dark and very sick. If you're into all that true crime stuff, you'll know some of the names involved.

Normally I don't have anything to do with this kind of thing; I don't even read up on it because it turns my stomach. It is the complete opposite of what I am all about, which is love and peace and white light. I know a lot of people don't want to face up to the fact that there is dark stuff like this going on, but in this world there is good and bad, black and white, dark and light. And for some reason I ended up becoming involved with very dark forces, starting with those portals at that house – my only guess is that because somehow I am able to help.

Sadly, there are a lot of victims who are trapped like those spirit people I found in the portal, because of the evil that has been done to them, and who need to be able to cross into the light. To start with we thought there were just a few, but it turns out it is much, much bigger than that. Getting those trapped souls out of the portal at the house proved to be the tip of the iceberg, and now I know it is the reason why I ended up becoming involved with this show. I am meant to be helping those souls.

I have been back to the States several times since then to work on more episodes of the show, which is no longer called *Haunted Hollywood*, because it's turning out to be about so much more than crime scenes or celebrity deaths in Tinseltown. At the moment, the show is called *Voices from the Grave*.

I have been to other places where I have been able to help spirit to cross over. I have seen how some of them died, and believe me it's horrific. I have also connected with the spirits of some of the truly evil people responsible for these deaths – like the serial killer who decided to hitch a ride with me that day when I was back in New Zealand. That freaks me out, let me tell you.

There is one case I can give a few details about, which involves the spirit of another serial killer, who went on a murderous spree in 1984 and 1985. His name was Richard Ramirez, but he was known as the Night Stalker. I am not exaggerating when I say Ramirez was pure evil. He was convicted of killing 13 people in the vicious Night Stalker attacks in California, and a nine-year-old girl in a separate incident.

Many of his crimes involved breaking into family homes, and shooting the men and raping the women, before making off with stolen goods. Sometimes he killed both husband and wife; on a few occasions his victims escaped with terrible injuries. Many of those who survived reported that he asked them questions and demanded they 'swear to Satan' that the answers given were true. Some of the other things he did to these poor people are so disgusting I cannot even hint at them, let alone give details. He was a monster.

The 25-year-old was eventually caught in August 1985, and found guilty at his trial four years later, and on 7 November 1989 was sentenced to death. He spent more than 23 years on death row, but never made it to the gas chamber – instead he died in 2013, aged 53, from complications due to lymphoma.

During one of my trips to LA I went with Lisa and the crew to do some filming at an old apartment building, which is said to be the most haunted place in the city. There have been lots of tragic deaths there since it was built, and it gained further notoriety after it was discovered to be one of the places where Richard Ramirez was living for much of the time he was killing and terrorising innocent people in 1985.

Just getting to the apartment building was scary in itself. It is in a really bad part of LA, known as Skid Row, which is probably one of the worst places I have ever been in my life. A lot of people there are on a drug called 'Zombie', which, as its name suggests, really messes you up; we were walking past people in the street who were convulsing on the ground and foaming at the mouth. As a Kiwi, when you see something like that your first reaction is to see whether they need help. That's what I wanted to do, anyway. But my bodyguard Steve – we mediums are assigned protection when we're working – stopped me.

'Don't touch them,' he warned. 'They'll kill you.'

Once we got in the building, I did manage to connect to Ramirez, but not in the room where he stayed while he was on his killing rampage. Instead he was in the power-grid room in the basement, and, man, trying to talk to him was an intense situation.

This is a good place to remind you that when I do a reading with someone in spirit, it's their soul I connect with. Sometimes they show me what they looked like when they were on this side of life so that I can describe them, and their family member will know it is them. There are times when I can see whole people in great detail, but on other occasions I might just see their profile or their glasses or their hair. Sometimes I don't see anything.

One thing that often happens is that the images I get from spirit don't always exactly match how the person I am reading for remembers them. For example, a woman getting a reading with her grandma might think of her as she was before she died – old, hunched-over and wrinkled. But Granny might show me an image of herself as she was 50 years earlier – young, pretty and vibrant. That's how her soul wants to be seen.

When I came across Richard Ramirez in that basement, I didn't see him as young or old, healthy or sick with cancer. In fact I didn't even see him as human. He was a demon. I don't really know how to describe it other than to say it was petrifying. He was screeching at me. This was the spirit of a cold-blooded killer who took the lives of 14 people because in accordance with his satanic beliefs he wanted to keep them as his slaves in the afterlife.

But I couldn't show fear. I recalled what I had told my daughter, Jade, when I was teaching her what to do if a dog ever started to go at her. 'Stand your ground and show no fear,' I'd told her. It's the same with demonic forces. And in this instance I knew I was protected, because as I went in I had called on my angels and my spirit people to help me.

These are serious matters that you don't muck around with. I have incredible spiritual support and I have learned to deal with this sort of thing, but everyone else should steer clear. Never, ever go looking for this kind of dark energy – that means no séances and no ouija boards – and if you ever encounter anything that is negative and scary, say your prayers, ask spirit to surround you with protective white light, and get the hell out of there.

So, we had wondered whether there was anything we could learn from Ramirez about all of these linked evil things that had been going on in LA, and he did end up giving us potential clues about other cases we were working on. That's about as much as I can reveal at the moment, other than to say that it was an intense encounter and I am glad I don't end up in situations like that every day.

Freaky stuff

There has been a whole heap of other freaky stuff that has happened every time I have gone to LA to work on the show. Once I was channelling a murder victim and I ended up passing out. I actually stopped breathing for a moment, and Karen, the forensic consultant on the show, was about to give me CPR because she couldn't find my pulse. But thankfully I took a deep breath and came around. Lisa would have called 911, except we were in the pitch black and she couldn't find her phone.

Another time one of the other mediums, Maryne, was involved in a situation that became so overwhelming that Lisa called time on the shoot and got everyone to leave. When we were outside Maryne said she felt like she was being attacked, that spirit was literally clawing at her. 'It feels like they are all over me,' she said.

'It's all right, mate, I've got you covered,' I told her. I stood behind her, putting myself between her and whatever was doing this to her. 'You can't touch her,' I told them.

Another time, Maryne again felt like she was clawed on the back of her neck, and you could actually see the marks. And at the apartment building she felt like she'd been struck on the head, and a bump could be seen forming on her skull.

Then there was the experience that left Lisa and two crew members just about packing themselves, to put it bluntly. During that first day in the doctor's house, after I had closed down one of the two portals and we got the hell out of there, Lisa decided to go back into the basement to get a shot of a big old spooky-looking furnace. While she was there, she heard a very scary growling noise, which freaked her out, and she took off in a hurry.

But then she realised she had to go back to do an 'idiot check': go around the property to make sure everything was locked up, and that we hadn't left any gear behind. Because she'd heard that growl, she decided to take two crew members with her to the basement. They had checked that everything was okay and were leaving together, when the crew member coming up the stairs in last place began screaming, 'Get off me! Get off me!'

He later said he had heard a scratching sound, and then something grabbed his shoulders and tried to pull him back down the stairs. He ploughed past the other crew member, who was female, and grabbed Lisa, using her like a shield to protect himself against this spirit that was holding onto him. They all fell down in a heap, and it ended up being one of those situations where they were so terrified that they broke into hysterical laughter. Even so, they got out pretty quickly after that.

I've got to know this guy and he is an awesome dude, and not the sort to normally barge his way past two women. This was obviously a special circumstance! As a result, he has been given the nickname Demon Bait, and it's going to take a while for him to live that down. Thankfully he could see the funny side later, but for a moment there he had the living daylights scared out of him.

So yeah, there have been lots of spooky happenings going on, but the safety of everyone working on the show is a top priority and we all have each other's backs – literally. The crew are really tight-knit and have become like a family. They are very cool people who are doing an awesome job, under what are often very difficult circumstances.

Since working on *Voices from the Grave* I have become especially close to my bodyguard, Steve. He's a fantastic guy and we have a great laugh together. I keep nagging him to come out to New Zealand on holiday, and I can't wait to take him fishing on my boat.

I have also developed really strong bonds with Lisa and Karen Smith – the ex-homicide detective who was hired to work on the show around the same time I was, and who has since married Lisa. These two women are just incredible, and being asked to be part of this journey with them has been a privilege. I feel lucky to also be their friend. It has been interesting to hear about their spiritual backgrounds, and what it's been like working on the show from their point of view. I'll let them share that with you in the next couple of chapters.

But just let me say, Lisa and Karen: you are both outstanding human beings and I feel so proud to know you.

CHAPTER 6

The director

When I was first contacted out of the blue by Lisa Statman, I have to admit I was a little wary. I'd previously been asked to appear on a US version of *Sensing Murder*, and, after asking me all about the Kiwi series, the people making it went ahead and shot it without me. I wasn't very impressed, although it sounds like I had a lucky escape – the show tanked.

Still, Lisa seemed above-board, and when she asked if we could Skype I thought, Why not? During what was essentially a job interview, I was flattered when she said that she was moved by how sincere and honest I was on *Sensing Murder*. That's important to me: I never try to be someone I am not, and I always try to be open and upfront about what I am getting – or not getting – from spirit.

As we were talking, I became aware of spirit around Lisa and I ended up doing a reading for her. The woman who came through, whose name was Patti, told me she was Lisa's partner, and she had died of breast cancer. Patti had children from a previous relationship, and thanked Lisa for caring for them after she died. It was a really emotional reading – they had clearly shared such a deep love.

I could tell that Patti had been one amazing lady on this side of life, and now that she was on the other side she had her wings.

What I didn't know until later was that Patti was the sister of Hollywood actress Sharon Tate, who was murdered by the Charles Manson gang in 1969. Their mother, Doris, had gone on to be a tireless campaigner for the rights of victims and their families – she was the first person to read out a victim impact statement in a Californian court – and Patti had carried on her work helping bereaved families after Doris died.

Lisa has written a book, *Restless Souls: The Sharon Tate Family's Account of Stardom, Murder and a Crusade for Justice*, along with Patti's daughter Brie. Lisa is a great writer, but TV and film are her first loves, and over the years she has worked as an assistant director or second-unit director on a whole load of hit movies and shows, including *A Few Good Men*, *Free Willy*, *Ally McBeal* and *Kitchen Confidential*. She has also worked on the brilliant Emmy-award-winning sitcom *Modern Family* for a long time, stepping up in recent years to direct quite a few episodes.

Lisa is a highly intelligent but very humble person with a huge heart, and she's fascinating to talk to. And she is of course very open and sensitive to spirit. But it wasn't always that way. She was pretty sceptical about all that communicating with ghosts stuff, until a spooky experience changed her mind . . .

Lisa says

When Patti was dying of breast cancer in 2000, she wrote a letter to her children and gave it to me to pass on to them after she was gone. When the time came for me to do that, I went to look for the letter and couldn't find it anywhere. I ripped my house apart three times looking for it with no luck, then a friend said to me, 'Why don't you call a medium?'

I'd heard of psychics but not mediums, and I didn't really understand the concept of what was involved. But by that stage I was willing to try anything to find the letter (what kind of jerk loses the last letter from someone to their children?), so I went to see a woman who worked as a medium.

She told me lots of things about Patti that couldn't have been just good guesses, and then she said, 'What's your question? I know you have a question.'

I asked where the letter was, and the woman then asked me a bunch of questions, starting with 'Did Patti like birdhouses?' The answer to that was yes. She asked where the birdhouses were at our house, and I told her that they were all over the place. That didn't seem to help.

Next she asked whether Patti got massages when she was really sick, and to check where the massages had taken place.

'It was the bedroom, and I have checked every inch of it,' I said.

Then she asked whether there was a statue in the house of people holding hands. I said no.

Her final question was: 'Did Patti wear a lot of hats?' Yes, she did. 'Wherever the hats are, the letter is going to be below them,' she told me.

On the drive home I was kind of exhilarated, because I felt like I had connected with Patti. The medium knew things she couldn't possibly have known without connecting with Patti in some way. Yet I still didn't know exactly where the letter was.

When I got home, I went straight to the master bedroom. There was a tapping noise, and I looked through the glass doors to see a birdhouse outside swinging in the wind. Then I looked straight ahead, and above our bed was a circle of angels all holding hands, which I had never really paid any attention to.

I went into the walk-in closet, where Patti's hats were. Sitting at the back of the closet, under the hats, was the backpack that was Patti's go-to bag when she had to spend time in hospital. I had already searched it, but I thought, What the heck. I took the hats off, opened the backpack, and there was the letter, lying right on top.

I realised that to help me find the letter, Patti had taken the medium from one point to the next to the next until I got to the backpack. From that moment on, I was a believer.

I thought if it's true that people can communicate with the other side, can I learn to do it? Patti had left behind three children, and I was raising two of them. If I could communicate with her, she could continue to have a say in what was happening in her children's lives.

That led me down a spiritual path of meditation and learning how to communicate with spirit.

THE DIRECTOR

A passion for the paranormal

Voices from the Grave came about because I wanted to make a TV show I was passionate about. I love directing half-hour comedies, but, as blessed as I am to do that, it's not really my passion. At the time my son had just become a police officer, and he was so excited about his job he would get up two hours early every day to iron his uniform. He couldn't wait to get to work, he loved it so much. I wanted to do something that made me feel that way.

So I started thinking: What makes me really excited? The first thing I thought of was paranormal stuff. The second was solving mysteries. And the third was being able to help people. I wanted to combine those three things – and that's how the show came about.

The idea was to get mediums to look into famous murder cases in Los Angeles, and I set about putting together a really good team. I wanted the best of the best. I thought it was a good idea to have three mediums, and it was important that they worked differently from each other. To me, spirit are just like us in that there are some people they feel comfortable with and are happy to talk to, and there are others they are not so comfortable with. If we had three mediums who worked in different ways, that would give spirit more options to connect with someone.

I had Joe Perreta, who is American, and Maryne Hachey, who is Canadian, and I found Kelvin kind of by accident. I was looking for the US version of *Sensing Murder* on YouTube and instead I found the New Zealand series.

From the moment I saw him, I thought Kelvin was amazing.

I liked his empathy, his manner; in fact, I liked everything about him. And I felt drawn to him. Sometimes you feel like you know someone even if you have never met them; you can't explain why, but you feel as if you are meant to be close. It was that way with Kelvin.

After watching him on *Sensing Murder* I said to our casting director: 'I want this guy – can you find him in New Zealand?'

To start with, she had no luck. For about six months she kept saying, 'We can't find him: we've sent out multiple emails, we've tried everything, but we can't get hold of him.' Then all of a sudden, out of the blue, she said to me, 'We've found Kelvin.'

I interviewed all of the mediums by Skype, and I decided Patti would help me to figure out who I would work with. I said to her, 'I'm going to ask each of them if they sense anyone around me, and if you like this person, appear to them.'

I'd been talking to Kelvin for about half an hour when I said 'Do you see anyone around me?', and he immediately picked up on Patti. It was an amazing reading and I knew 100 percent that I wanted him on the show.

When I initially brought Kelvin to the United States, he had no idea there were two other mediums, and they didn't know about him either. We had a meet-and-greet dinner and it was interesting to watch the three of them together. I kept telling them, 'Listen, this isn't a contest, it isn't about who gets the most from spirit, it is about working as a team.' They got that.

There were other members of the team who were also crucial – our crew members who use the special equipment we take with us when we go into places like the doctor's house. One piece of equipment we use is what's known as structured-light-sensor (SLS) cameras. Basically, what they do is map when spirit energy is present, which shows up like a stick-figure in the camera. So, for instance, when Kelvin was pulling the spirits from the portal in the murder house to release them into the light, we could actually see them on camera going up through the ceiling. It was truly amazing.

Often Kelvin will be standing there and all of a sudden he will start talking to someone we can't see, until we look in the SLS camera. Then you can see the spirit stick-figure standing next to him. It is mind-blowing.

We also have static cameras which we put on infrared so that they have night vision. Spirit can show up on them as an orb, sparks of light, streaks and shadows moving about. Once we were in one location when the static camera picked up what is probably the most amazing footage ever caught. There were hundreds of these lights, it looked like an explosion. They left trails as spirit moved from one level of the house to another – you could see them going up the stairwell. In my inexperience I discounted this as dust. Later, when we had paranormal experts look at it, they explained that dust is seen on camera and moves very differently – almost like a light snow.

We also use audio equipment known as ghost boxes. These pick up and record sound from spirit. When Kelvin is communicating with spirit, to us it's a one-sided conversation as we can't hear what spirit is saying to him. But when we listen to the ghost box we can hear sounds, including voices. We've heard people getting hit, people screaming, people crying for help. We've had Kelvin say 'There's a demon in front of me', and on the ghost box we've heard a growl that sends a chill down your spine.

At one point Kelvin was talking to a woman in spirit as he was crossing her over into the light. When we listened to the ghost box we could hear a woman's voice saying, 'I'm here.' It was cool to know he'd got her into the light.

It is amazing to witness this, and also to be able to validate everything Kelvin is saying. He's not just talking to himself!

The other thing we do is bring in cadaver dogs. These dogs are specially trained to sniff out human remains, and they are extraordinarily smart and sensitive. For example, they hit on an area right underneath that explosion of orbs that we could see on the static camera. One dog, Piglet, had a pretty extreme reaction. Her handler could tell that she was picking up on something negative, and even the handler could feel it.

We also took the dogs to the doctor's house to see if they would pick up on any of the things Kelvin had said happened. The dogs were alerting — or picking up on the scent of human remains — all over the place. Down in the basement one of them went off: he was literally climbing the walls trying to source the smell he had picked up on. He got to where Kelvin said the portal was, and he stopped cold, lay down and stretched out, frozen. He wouldn't move. Then all of a sudden he jerked his head back, like he was warding off a blow. That had never happened before.

As we were going through the house with the dogs, we were using the SLS camera, and when the dogs were going off we could see spirit all around them. You have to wonder, were they picking up on the smell of physical death, or were they sensing spirit?

Down to spirit

Making this show really has been about teamwork. Everyone on the team connected instantly, and we're all on the same page when it comes to helping the victims. The amazing thing is there are no egos, which is pretty incredible in Hollywood.

I feel that not only was I meant to find Kelvin and work with him, but the whole team was meant to be together, and spirit was responsible for that. I found everyone within about two hours of starting to look for people I thought would be good for the show (although it then took months to get hold of Kelvin). I'm thankful to spirit for bringing us together – the mediums, the crew, the cadaver dogs and their handlers, and of course Karen.

CHAPTER 7

The detective

When it comes to tough jobs, being a cop in America is right up there with the toughest of them. They see some pretty horrific and gruesome things, and they never know when someone is going to pull a gun on them. Their stress levels must be off the chain.

Karen Smith was a detective in the Jacksonville Sheriff's Office in Florida – a state she describes as 'the crazy capital of the United States' – for 11 years, and a training officer for three. During that time she worked 20,000 cases, including 500 death investigations, which ranged from suicides and accidental deaths through to homicides. She became known for her phenomenal ability to solve cases, and when she retired from her job six years ago she left the police force with only two cold cases to her name. Karen was so awesome that lawyers or other police departments would often contact her, asking for help.

Karen has a background in science. Along with a degree in criminal justice, she has a master's in pharmacy, majoring in forensic science. She stopped a year short of gaining her PhD when she moved to California. She went on to become a forensic expert, and is particularly skilled when it comes to the analysis of bloodstain patterns.

Over the years Karen has designed and taught courses on subjects like advanced crime scene investigation, analysis of bloodstain patterns on clothing, and clandestine grave detection. She was a consultant at the National Forensic Academy in Tennessee, has published two scientific papers and a textbook chapter, and lectures on forensic science and criminal justice at the University of Florida and Florida Gulf Coast University.

Since retiring as a serving police officer, she has become a consultant, working on cold cases, giving talks and appearing on TV shows and in documentaries to share her expert opinion. I told you she's an outstanding human being!

Thanks to her expertise, she was hired by Lisa to work on what was then called *Haunted Hollywood*. The first time I met her was in the middle of the very intense situation that went down at the doctor's house, when she turned up to do some filming.

Until then, Karen had always been what she calls a 'healthy sceptic'. She had an open mind, but coming from a science and a police background she needed hard evidence before she'd believe anything.

Although it wasn't planned, the day we first met I did a reading for her that really opened her eyes. She was Miss I-Don't-Trust-Anyone-Especially-Not-Freaky-Dudes-From-New-Zealand when we first met, but after our conversation I could see a shift in her. Not only has she come to understand that spirit is very real, but it has dawned on her that, throughout her career, spirit has been giving her a helping hand. All of those cases she was able to solve when nobody else could . . . Guess who she has to thank?

> ## *Karen says*
>
> I'm very new to all this stuff with spirit: I'm still waking up, as they say. I'm steeped in science, and so for me it has always been about formulating a hypothesis, looking for evidence and working from that.
>
> When Lisa interviewed me about being on the show, she asked how I felt about working with mediums. That was something I had never done as a police officer. Sure, I'd heard of police departments using mediums when a case had gone cold and they'd run out of leads. But I'd never heard of a medium actually leading police to a body – which Kelvin has done twice.
>
> Still, I'm the sort of person who has an open mind, and I won't shut things off without looking into it for myself. So I went into working on the show open to whatever happened, yet with a healthy scepticism about the whole thing, because I didn't understand how mediums worked. I found out pretty quickly!
>
> The first investigation was at the doctor's house, and I was working my way through the forensics there when Kelvin said to me, 'I have someone coming through for you.'
>
> I said, 'Really?' And he went, 'Yeah, Bob, Robert, Bobby . . . Who's Bob?'
>
> I wasn't sure to start with. I had a second cousin called Bobby, but I didn't think he would come through.

Then Kelvin said, 'This guy's African-American, and he has got the most incredible smile I have ever seen.' Instantly, I knew who he was talking about.

My friend Bobby was on the force with me, and we'd worked together on undercover prostitution deployment. I played a hooker and would walk the streets to get a 'john', who we would then arrest. Bobby would be in a van parked behind a building, and if anything went down he had my back.

One night a man pulled a gun on me, and I ran to the van. Bobby had thrown the door open and was squatting down with his arms wide open, saying, 'Run to Bobby – come on baby, let's go!' I dived into the van and he took off like a bat out of hell. We chased this guy up the road and arrested him. Bobby saved my life that day.

Sadly, Bobby died in the line of duty – he had a heart attack while driving. He was crossing a bridge when it happened, and he had the presence of mind not to careen into oncoming traffic. Instead he deliberately crashed the car into a wall. He potentially saved other lives as he was dying.

Kelvin said to me: 'Bobby wants you to know that he is still looking out for you.' I lost it. I broke down in tears, and I remember Lisa throwing a toilet roll at me because I was blubbering. But I couldn't help it. I was dumbfounded.

I said to Kelvin, 'You've got to be kidding me.'

He said, 'No, I'm not. Bobby's your protector.'

It was a wonderful moment, and it completely opened my eyes.

Since then, from what I have seen and experienced working with Kelvin and the other mediums, I know that spirit exists. It's real. I have seen what Kelvin is able to do and the information he gets, and there is only one place it is coming from.

I think it's up to each of us to decide what we believe and to come to a personal acceptance of what happens when we die. You can label it how you want to, but for me there's no denying it anymore.

It has been an eye-opening experience, because the paranormal is the complete opposite of what I have been used to. I am used to tangible evidence – things I can touch, feel, taste, smell and see. Now I am dealing with something that I can't explain, but which is still giving me evidence to work with. I've just had to accept it.

I've been able to meld my scientific brain with my spiritual side in a way that makes sense to me. As a scientist, I can say that there's 95 percent of the universe that we don't understand. We know what is going on with 5 percent; the rest is a mystery. But just because we don't have the science to back up what's there, or the tools to measure it, that doesn't mean it's not there. It just means we don't get it.

And we do have some ways of measuring or recording spirit activity. For example, those cadaver dogs were certainly picking up on something in the doctor's basement. At some stage there had been dead bodies there. We have cameras and ghost boxes that pick up spirit. You can hear and see them.

The ghost boxes are amazing. I often have experiences I call a 'headphone throw' moment. I will be listening through headphones and hear the sound spirit make, and be so blown away that I'll take off my headphones and throw them across the desk. Being still new to all of this, I'll get up and say, 'I can't handle this.'

One headphone-throw moment happened when I was at home reviewing footage we'd shot and audio we'd recorded. As I listened to the ghost box I heard something that I can't go into detail about at this stage. But I can say that it was so distinct, and so frightening, that I threw off my headphones and broke down in tears.

Then I ran outside into the backyard, squatted down next to the house and said out loud: 'I don't know if I am doing the right thing – please somebody send me a sign that this is right.'

Out of nowhere, a gorgeous white butterfly suddenly appeared. It stopped right in front of my face, about two inches from my nose, and flapped its wings for a good 10 seconds.

I instantly calmed down, and said, 'Well, okay. Okay then.' I knew it was someone coming to comfort me and tell me that everything was all right.

Before all this happened, if a butterfly had just appeared in front of me when I was upset I wouldn't have paid it any attention. I definitely wouldn't have seen it as a sign. But in that moment, that was exactly how I took it, and it helped. It was an enlightening moment for me.

A helping hand

One of the things that has come out of me stepping into this new realm and working with Lisa, Kelvin and everyone else on the show is that I not only believe that spirit are there and are real, but I now understand that spirit have been assisting me in my work for many years.

Kelvin and the others have said to me: 'Karen, spirit have been helping you with your investigations this whole time, whether you knew it or not. You're sensitive to spirit, and you need to embrace it.'

It has taken me three years to understand and accept that I have been guided by spirit. I previously had no idea.

Now when I look back at some of the things I did, and the cases I was able to solve, I can't help thinking: Why did nobody else find what I found? I was working with a lot of really intelligent, experienced people, but I was the one who was closing case after case. I was the one finding things that other people had missed.

I started getting a lot of phone calls from the state attorney saying, 'I have this case . . . can you come and have a look at it?' Inevitably, I would find some piece of evidence that had been overlooked by everyone else. All of these cold cases were closing because of me, and it was crazy.

One of those cases involved a car crash. A pick-up truck containing two young men had smashed through a three-rail fence, and one of the guys died. The other one was found standing by the passenger door when everyone got there, and said he hadn't been driving. Over a year after the incident, the prosecutor asked me to meet him at his office and said he needed me to figure out whether, based on forensic evidence, that was correct.

The board from the fence that had struck the young man and killed him had been put into evidence after being examined in the lab. It had blood patterns on it that the attorney wanted me to look at. I checked out the blood and there was nothing unusual about it. Then something told me to take a look at the other end of the board. So I unwrapped it, got out my magnifying glass, and found a single hair sticking out of one of the shards of wood. It hadn't been noticed before, obviously. I plucked it out, packaged it up and said to the prosecutor, 'You need to send this off to the lab. I think it is going to belong to the victim.'

Finding that hair started a chain of events that led to me looking into where on his head the guy had been struck by the board, and at the blood spatters on the clothes that he and the other guy in the car had been wearing. To cut a long story short, I worked out that the blood stains on the dead man's clothes pointed to the fact that he was the passenger, and the guy who survived had been driving.

As a result, the driver was convicted and got 15 years for DUI (drink-driving) manslaughter. Finding that one hair at the other end of the board had started the whole cycle of getting the evidence that led to being able to place the right person in the driver's seat, and then get the conviction. Something had compelled me to look at the other end of the board, and I don't know if it was my intuition or if it was the spirit of the young guy who had died telling me to do it. To me, it doesn't matter one way or the other, as long as the correct person is charged with the crimes they have committed.

Ask any cop worth their salt and they will tell you that they often have intuitive thoughts, or what we call a sixth sense. If something is about to go down, the hairs on the back of their neck will stand up, or they will get a funny feeling.

THE DETECTIVE

> Now I know that the sixth sense cops have is the same thing that Kelvin and the other mediums tap into. I trusted that sense when I was in uniform and on the street; I trusted it when it came to looking for evidence. I could never understand why I would latch onto information that others had missed, but now I have put two and two together, and it adds up to spirit.

CHAPTER 8

TV, tears and taking a chance

See what I mean about Lisa and Karen? They're two very special people, and completely dedicated to *Voices from the Grave*. I would love to be able to tell you more about what we've been doing for the show, because it is going to blow everyone's minds, but I can't until it has screened.

At the moment a screening date has not been set. This is partly because more work needs to be done on the programme. Also, Lisa is being very careful when it comes to putting this show out in public. We need the right TV executives who will agree to let her run the show as she wants it to run. Because the show hasn't turned out as Lisa had initially thought it would, people can't quite grab the concept. It has gone from looking at cases of famous Hollywood deaths, like those of actresses Marilyn Monroe and Natalie Wood, and actor Bob Crane (who starred in *Hogan's Heroes*), and haunted houses, through to uncovering this ring of terrible crimes and trying to help the dead victims, who have been unable to cross over.

Because it is an incredibly sensitive subject, we have to make sure everything is done properly, and that everyone working on the show is kept safe. This is Lisa's main priority: safety.

Yes, a TV programme is about entertaining and informing people, but there's a lot more to this show. Lisa feels a big responsibility to the victims we're trying to help, in the same way I always felt a responsibility to spirit I connected with on *Sensing Murder*. At the end of the day, spiritual work boils down to helping others.

Right from when I first started working on *Sensing Murder*, and now carrying on with *Voices from the Grave*, my aim has been to bring closure and peace to victims and their families. Being able to help a murder victim who has been through a terrible experience is a privilege and is spiritually rewarding.

I am so pleased *Voices from the Grave* is emphasising the victims, because so often they get forgotten. If someone is caught and convicted, often it is that person whose name and story become known and gets all the media attention. Let's honour the memory of those who have lost their lives, not focus on the perpetrators.

Karen says

Along with friends and family, there is another group of people who never forget the victims, and that's the police officers who work the case. They remember everything, and it is especially hard to let go when you haven't been able to get the person responsible locked away.

I really wish police departments would give someone of Kelvin's ability and proven track record the opportunity to help them out. When you have a case that is going nowhere, when there are no leads, no witnesses and you have nothing left to follow up on, what's the harm in calling in a medium?

I realise that if a medium is able to tell you something that leads to an arrest, that information won't be admissible in court. However, if it leads you to tangible evidence that *is* admissible in court, like a murder weapon or DNA, then it doesn't matter how you found it. What matters is that you did find it, and it could be what convicts the perpetrator.

When a medium leads police to evidence, the police should work the scene just the same as any other investigator would with any other piece of information. They have to stick to the evidence, and follow leads to a factual conclusion. There are no free passes.

I think a lot of cops are worried about what their colleagues will say, what the attorneys will say and how it will play out in court if they reveal that a medium led them to the body. The judicial system does not give credence to mediums. It's time to get over that. Just follow up on what the medium tells you, get out there and solve the case, and bring some justice to the victim and closure to their family.

One of the worst things you have to do as a cop is go to a family and tell them someone they love has been murdered. You hear that horrible, guttural wail of 'No, not my son, not my daughter', and you know that it is incumbent on you to do everything you can to bring justice. So why wouldn't you want to use everything available to you to do that?

I retired with two cold cases that I couldn't solve, and they haunt me. You don't let cases like that go just because you are no longer wearing a badge. They're in the back of your mind all the time, and every so often you think about the victims and wonder: What did I miss? What could I have done?

I would love nothing more than to get my hands on those cases again and see whether Kelvin or our other mediums can pick up anything that might be of value. We might think we have exhausted all of the leads, but the thing is, there is evidence, we just haven't found it. A medium might be able to make all the difference. Why not take a chance, and give them a shot?

Lisa says

I would love for this show to change how murder investigations are carried out. My goal is for people to watch it and see what we achieve when it comes to working out what happened, so that they become more open to using mediums. I don't know if I will see it in my lifetime, but wouldn't it be good if, after a murder is committed, the police, the forensic team and the medical examiner go in and do what they need to do, and then, instead of leaving it until all of the leads have dried up, a medium is brought in at the start of the investigation to see what they come up with?

They might be able to tell you what happened; who did it; where they are. Or all they might be able to do is give you a name – Tony, for example – and tell you they've seen a guy who is six foot two with red hair. That's a start. It can then be treated and investigated in the same way as information from any other witness. It doesn't mean the medium has to become a part of the court process. Hopefully there will be other evidence that points to Tony the redhead as the guilty person – phone records or forensics, for example.

I suspect all it will take for attitudes to change is one case that is solved with the help of a medium. Just one brave detective who is prepared to work with someone like Kelvin and follow through on what they are told. They need to view the medium's insights in the same way they look at evidence provided by cadaver dogs, or GPS, or CCTV cameras – they're just a different tool.

If there is just one case where a medium makes all the difference, then I think using them will take off and everyone will be doing it.

Karen says

As a cop I would work with any information I got, follow up every lead and investigate every single thing, no matter how insignificant it seemed. I thought I worked hard when I was a cop, but, to be honest, working on this show has become the toughest thing I have ever done.

I really hope it opens people's eyes and makes them think about spirit, and what people like Kelvin and our other mediums can do. if you just watch the show for a few minutes, it might change your whole perception.

It has truly been a privilege to work with Kelvin and to have become a close friend of his. He is a kind and genuine soul, who wants nothing but good for everyone around him.

Lisa says

One of Kelvin's special skills is his ability to handle the negative stuff. I think that's down to his experience and everything he has been through in his life, coupled with his entire belief system. When we started the series, I had no idea that we'd be hitting this truly negative stuff. In fact, if I'd known then what I know now, I would never have taken the team into the doctor's house, because it turned out to be so much bigger and darker than we could have imagined. We certainly didn't go looking for any of this: it found us.

I remember standing in the basement of the house the first time when things were going crazy, and Kelvin saying to me, 'You realise this was all planned out years before we met, don't you? We are all supposed to be here, and we all have a mission.'

I didn't really get it at the time; I do now.

All of our mediums are extremely talented people who have special gifts they use in different ways. The spiritual journey Kelvin has been on and his life experiences enable him to deal with the evil we've encountered with great authority, knowledge and strength.

I didn't fly Kelvin over when we investigated another house that was said to be haunted, because we were really only going to test out different ghost boxes and see what we picked up. But when we were there we found more negative energy, and we figured out that it was tied to the first investigation at the doctor's house. Realising the depth of what has been going on with this group of people is really scary, and I feel better when Kelvin is there. He makes us feel protected.

So when things get intense, and I see it affecting Kelvin, who is the strongest of us, that's when I tend to worry. If he seems to be looking at something and then says 'You don't want to know what I am seeing', I know we are in a really bad place.

But even though it has gotten darker and scarier than we could have imagined, there have been amazing moments that make it all worthwhile. For example, it has been miraculous to witness the occasions when Kelvin has been able to cross people who were being held in the afterlife into the light. We could actually see it on our cameras.

Yes, the programme has to entertain, and will show how Kelvin and our other mediums are able to communicate with people who have passed on. But our core intent is to help spirit, and being able to help has become the most important part of the show.

I think that once the series screens, people will see the two sides to Kelvin: the guy who can find out what happened in cases that are a mystery, and the person who can take care of evil when that needs to be done, too.

Karen says

One of the places we filmed in was the scene of a murder that, even though it was fairly famous, we didn't know a huge amount about. Lisa and I went to scout the location a few days beforehand; we took photos and everything seemed fine, squeaky clean.

However, it was a different story when we went back to

film. I felt terrible, I couldn't concentrate, I was nauseous and anxious, and my palms were sweaty. I was shaking like a leaf, and I couldn't understand what was going on, because there was no reason on the planet for me to feel like that. I'd been to lots of other locations where people had been murdered and I'd been fine, and I'd had no problem when we'd scouted this place.

I got to a stairwell, but couldn't go down it; something was telling me that bad things had happened there. It was a really horrible feeling.

Kelvin arrived shortly afterwards, and the moment he walked in he started experiencing exactly the same symptoms as me. It was bad for both of us. Later on it got so terrible I had to run out. I don't know if it was my anxiety, or if I was being attacked, or what, but I had to get out of there. My legs went out from under me as I was going down the stairs, and I barely made it out to the back patio.

Kelvin immediately took me off the property, and we sat on the kerbside across the street. We talked for ages, and he said there were some things that had gone down in that house that we hadn't known about, and it was really serious. In fact later on that was where he went down after an encounter with the victim and stopped breathing, and I thought I was going to have to do CPR on him.

It was interesting that I had picked up on the negative energy, and I think that was my moment of realising that I'm sensitive to spirit.

I also felt this weird link to Kelvin because we were both experiencing the same physical symptoms. It was a real bonding moment, and it is also when I realised that Kelvin was going to protect me and the team. I knew he would not let anything bad happen, and I felt safe with him.

Lisa says

Kelvin amazes me all the time. Often he will say things and I'll think: What are you talking about? That doesn't mean anything to me. But then further down the track what he has said or done will suddenly make sense. I'll be reviewing footage we've shot, or something will come to light and I'll realise: Oh, Kelvin said that. He knew about this.

One case we've been working on has been pushed way forward because of things he has told us. In another case, he has given us a description of a killer, someone who has not been caught, and if he turns out to be right, I am going to freak out.

I realised just how incredible his ability is after that first day at the doctor's house. Before everything happened in the basement with the portals, he had connected with the wife, who had been murdered by her husband. I had seen photos of her, so I knew what she looked like – she was what I would call a handsome woman, with short dark hair. So when he started talking about a gorgeous woman with long blonde hair, I was confused. All I could think was that maybe at some stage the wife had grown her hair and dyed it blonde. But as he was being filmed walking around the house talking to spirit, quite a lot of what he said didn't make sense either. It didn't seem to relate to the doctor's crimes. At the time I thought, Oh well, maybe I will figure it out later.

The day after the investigation, Kelvin came to my house for the first time. It had belonged to Patti's family, and there is a portrait of Sharon Tate hanging in the living room. Kelvin pointed at it and said, 'Who's that?'

I told him it was Patti's sister Sharon.

'That's the other woman who was at the house yesterday,' he said. 'She was looking out the window when I arrived, and I spoke to her throughout the day.'

I couldn't believe it. 'You're kidding, right?' I asked him.

'Nope,' he said. 'She was there.'

I couldn't help wondering why Sharon's spirit would show up at that house, of all places, and then hijack Kelvin as he did the walk-through.

So I went back and watched the footage that had been shot, and there are clearly parts where he is not talking to the doctor's wife, he is talking to someone else, and to me, from what he said, it is clearly Sharon. I had been so focused on the murder-suicide that he could have said Sharon's name and I probably wouldn't have registered that she was there with him. That was one of those Kelvin moments that completely blows my mind.

He constantly does things you don't expect. For instance, we were in the middle of working with the cadaver dogs on a case when Kelvin said, 'I'm crying, I don't know why I am crying.' Then he turned around to one of the dog-handlers and said, 'I think I'm picking up on your dad.' It wasn't anything to do with what we were working on, but her father was coming through, so off they went for a while and he proceeded to give her a reading from her dad. That's Kelvin for you.

Another time he told us he couldn't get that song from the

movie *Mary Poppins* out of his mind – the one about a spoonful of sugar helping the medicine go down. A while later we went to a location that had music playing on loudspeakers, and that exact song was playing as we arrived, and kept playing the whole time we were there.

Karen did some research later, because she can't help herself, and found out that this particular place has a library of 12,000 songs. So we had a one in 12,000 chance of hearing the song Kelvin had been talking about . . . and we did. This is what he does.

And then there was a moment that to me was personally amazing, and I will never forget it. Kelvin was staying at our place, and one day, out of nowhere, he started singing the song 'You Are My Sunshine' to me. He got to a certain point, then he said, 'You know the rest of the words.'

I said to him: 'Are you kidding me?'

He added, 'I don't know why I am singing this.'

I did, and I knew what he meant about knowing the rest of the words.

When Patti was dying, she got to the stage where she was still alert enough to cock her head if we wanted to give her a kiss, but I knew it was time for her to go. She hung onto life for days in this state, and I couldn't understand why. I wondered if it was because she felt like I wasn't able to release her. So I started singing 'You Are My Sunshine' to her, but instead of singing 'Please don't take my sunshine away' I changed the words so I was asking for 'them' to come and take her over, to set her free. I was giving her permission to go.

I can't carry a tune to save my life, so I sang it very softly in her ear in case, God forbid, anyone else heard me. She died

> two days later, and I've never told anyone else about it, not even Karen.
>
> So when Kelvin started singing that song I began blubbering like an idiot. It wasn't because I was sad, but because nobody else in the world, other than Patti and me, knew about that. Only two people could have told him what 'You Are My Sunshine' meant, and I know I didn't.

Moving pictures

There have certainly been a few tears shed while I've been working in the States. But it hasn't all been scary or sad. There have been some fun moments, too.

For example, I laughed over an incident that had Karen and Lisa freaking out the last time I was there, when I was staying with them at their home, which has a lot of history. It used to belong to Patti and Sharon's parents, who Lisa knew well, and there are photos of the Tate family hanging on the walls. One day I was looking at a photo when I saw it move. I swear on my life, I saw the hand of the dad, PJ, come out and move the photo. And I'm telling you, it moved a lot.

It couldn't have been due to anything like a breeze coming in a window and blowing it. The thing about the pictures in that house is that Lisa is really pedantic about them: not only does she put them up using a spirit level – no pun intended! – to make sure they are straight, she then sticks them to the wall with a putty they call earthquake tape. The area gets a lot of earthquakes, and the putty stops the photos from falling off the wall. Once it is in place, you cannot move those pictures.

But when I was there, that picture moved every day. Lisa and

Karen were like 'Whoa!', but to me it was just a sign that these beautiful souls are still with us, and they are just telling us 'Hey, we're here, we've got your back, there's no need to worry about anything.' I think that's cool – and I have to admit it was a bit of a buzz watching Karen and Lisa lose it!

Lisa reckons she has known for a long time that these special people are with her in spirit in the house, but she had laid down some ground rules with them. She'd told them: 'I love you, and I want you here, but you're not allowed to move stuff and you're not allowed to show yourself because I'll need to change my underwear!' But she thinks that because I was there, spirit wanted to make themselves known, and moving the picture was how they did it.

Stuff like that can be weird, but we need to remember that most of the time it is not a negative thing. Sure, I have been going on about haunted houses and scary things happening, and focusing on some really heavy stuff – but encounters with spirit aren't usually like that. For most of us, if strange things start happening, like items in your house moving unexpectedly, it's not bad. Don't panic: it's just your loved ones being friendly and saying, 'Hi, I'm here.' All you need to do is say 'hi' back.

CHAPTER 9

The Land of the Rising Sun

Just a couple of months after one of my mind-blowing trips to Los Angeles to work on *Voices from the Grave*, I found myself on another international flight, this time to Japan.

I had been invited to attend the annual Yashi Fair, which is a huge spiritual event, with mediums, psychics and healers from all over the world. I've travelled quite a bit, but when I arrived in Tokyo it was a real culture shock. My first time in Los Angeles had been a big eye-opener – you've got to remember that I'm a country boy from the Waikato and now live in a quiet semi-rural location in the Bay of Islands – but Tokyo was next level. With all its noise and traffic and lights and people, it felt even more overwhelming to me.

To be honest, the timing of the Japanese trip wasn't brilliant.

LISTEN TO SPIRIT

I was still processing what had happened in LA, and, after all the horrible stuff that had gone down there, I had been left with spiritual residue, which I was still trying to clear. I was really tired, and when I got to Tokyo it felt quite scary. Later on, when I had a day off, I did go out and see some of the sights, including a spectacular temple, and I enjoyed myself. In fact, I would love to take my daughter Jade there one day to experience how different it is.

But to start with I didn't want to leave my hotel room, even though it was so tiny you would not have been able to swing a cat. The bathroom was the size of my pantry, which is not big. The shower was so small I couldn't get in it, and to go to the loo I had to squeeze myself in backwards and sit with my legs out the door!

I couldn't make the TV work because the instructions were in Japanese, and when I did finally go outside it was 40-something degrees and I instantly melted. It was a bit of a nightmare, to be honest. But I was there to do a job, and to have a new experience, so I told myself: 'KC, just get on with it.'

I did workshops, live shows and private readings at the fair, although the language difference proved a challenge. Once I had made the connection with spirit a reading would go pretty much as normal, with me getting images through my third eye, like a little movie running in my mind. However, as I can't speak Japanese I couldn't understand what was being said, but if it was important my spirit people – my family and my angels – would translate for me. Then the messages I got from spirit had to be translated from English into Japanese for the client by an interpreter. This seemed to take ages: I'd simply say 'I've got an elderly man here, I think it's your grandad', and two minutes later the interpreter would still be talking. Sometimes I got the feeling that they weren't necessarily telling the clients exactly what I was saying.

After a while, when I was doing private readings, I realised the easiest thing to do was to write things down. So I would listen to spirit and watch the pictures in my mind for a few minutes, write down what I had seen and heard in a long paragraph, and give that to the interpreter to read to the client. Then I'd wait for them to stop talking so I could get more messages and write them down.

This meant I was having to switch in and switch out again, which was hard. I really had to concentrate, and there were times when I wasn't sure where I'd got to and if it was my turn to speak or not. It was really tricky.

The readings were interesting nevertheless. I found that there is a lot of pressure on people in Japan to be perfect, to do exceptionally well at school and in their jobs. As a result, suicide is not uncommon, and I was shocked to hear that there's even a forest where people go to kill themselves. Apparently if you commit suicide in your home it brings shame on your family, so people go to this forest.

From what I saw, people also get very stressed over making decisions. I certainly felt that with one private reading I did. The lady basically wanted me to tell her what school her child should be sent to, according to spirit. She pulled six different school prospectuses out of her bag and said: 'Which one?'

I was thinking, Are you serious?

'Why can't you make up your mind?' I asked her. 'Why do I have to take ownership of this?'

'Because it is very important,' she said.

'If I tell you which one spirit is saying, you're not going to like it.'

'Please choose,' she said. 'Please tell me.'

So I did as she asked: I looked through the prospectuses and I asked spirit which one the woman's child should go to. The reply I got was: 'There are another six booklets in her bag – it's one of them.'

When I told the interpreter that the woman needed to get the other prospectuses out of her bag, the client was stunned. She looked at me as if to say 'How on earth do you know they are in there?' Nevertheless, she got them out, and spread them on the table. I looked through them, and her family in spirit indicated which school they thought the child should go to.

But when I told the lady, she said, 'Oh no, I don't like that one.' She proceeded to argue with me about it – in fact she was arguing with her dead grandmother and father. I couldn't believe it: she nagged me to point a school out to her, but refused to listen when it wasn't what she wanted to hear.

I sat there thinking: What am I doing here? This is not me.

Luckily, not all my readings were like that, but there were times when it was definitely a struggle.

A delightful daughter

When I wasn't working, I would go around the venue having a look at what else was going on. That was a revelation. There were obviously a lot of reputable people there doing good things, but there were also people who were manipulating the Japanese customers. In one place I watched someone from the UK telling the local people that they had aliens living inside them, and to get rid of the aliens they would need to buy the products the person was selling. I thought that was disgraceful.

For me, the Japanese trip wasn't really working out the way I thought it would, and there were times when I wondered whether attending had all been a big mistake.

But then I did a reading that made the whole trip worthwhile. The client was a really lovely lady who was so polite to the point that, when we were introduced, our bowing to each other got out of hand. Note to self: never try to out-bow a Japanese person, especially when you have a spinal injury.

The spirit who came through for her was her 10-year-old daughter. She was a lovely kid, all happy and super-excited and clapping her hands. She was talking so fast I could hardly keep up with her.

And then she showed me what had happened to her. Her mum had gone to pick her up from school, and, being so excitable and happy to see her mother, on this particular day she ran straight out across the road, into the path of a bus. That poor mother had watched her daughter going under the wheels of the bus.

I get emotional remembering it even now. As I was getting this information, I thought: How am I going to tell the mum that this is what I am being shown? I started to tell the interpreter, and she began choking up, even before she'd even said anything to the mother.

The interpreter said to me, 'How am I going to say this to her?'

'Welcome to my world,' I told her. 'You just have to get it out as sensitively as you can.'

The interpreter very reluctantly began to tell the woman what I had said about the girl getting hit by a bus, and as she did, the mum went from looking at the interpreter to staring at me, as if she was looking straight through me. It wasn't a bad thing; in fact, it was the opposite. In that moment we made a real connection, despite the language barrier.

Even with the challenges of working through an interpreter, it went on to be a wonderful reading. The little girl gave me so much detail to pass on to her mum, and it really was a truly beautiful experience, being able to connect this nice lady with the child she loved so much, and who had died in such tragic circumstances. All of us – me, the mum and the interpreter – ended up crying, it was so touching.

I felt like that reading was the whole point of me being in Japan. My purpose was to give that mother messages from her delightful daughter and to help her with her grief. If I had to deal with all the other stuff just to read for her, then so be it.

But as it turned out, there was another reason why spirit sent me to that fair in Japan. And that was to meet TJ Higgs.

The late, great Colin Fry

Among the other mediums at the Tokyo fair was a British woman called TJ Higgs. We met when we did a Q and A about spirit on stage together, and afterwards I got chatting to her and her partner, Stu, who is also her manager.

There was an instant rapport between us – and I'm including Stu here – which was pretty amazing. It solidified when we got talking and realised that not only had we both known the late British medium Colin Fry, but he had played a huge part in both of our careers.

For those of you who don't know who Colin is, he became famous around the world thanks to his TV show *6ixth Sense with Colin Fry*, which used to screen here on weekdays before the evening news. I was a huge fan, and in 2004, when I was just coming to grips with my ability to talk with dead people, I saved enough money to travel to England and also to Sweden, where I booked to do some courses at Colin's International College of Spiritual Science and Healing.

I was gutted when, just two weeks before I was due to fly out, the college emailed me to advise that, due to scheduling conflicts with filming his show in England, Colin wouldn't be available to teach in Sweden. I emailed back, saying I didn't think there was any point in coming if he wasn't going to be there. Colin then emailed me himself and apologised, which was nice of him. I replied saying I would still go to England because I had paid for my tickets, but I wouldn't be making the trip to Sweden. I then got an email back from him saying he would shout me tickets to his show.

I was beyond excited at the chance to see a man who was a

legend to me. The show was filmed at a theatre in Kent, and I was so overwhelmed that I was crying even before he came out on stage. He started to connect with spirit, and I couldn't believe it when my grandfather came through. He got me down on stage with him and all I could think was: I'm sitting next to Colin Fry! I don't remember a lot of what he said, but I do recall that it all made sense. I think he talked a lot about my son, Javan.

Afterwards I had to go to the green room to be interviewed for the TV programme about how the reading had gone, and while I was there I started reading for other people in the room. Nek minute, a woman who owned the TV company appeared with Colin, and said they'd noticed what I was doing.

'We would love for you to be a guest on the show,' she said.

So the next day there I was, this young guy from Ngaruawahia, New Zealand, doing readings on a TV show presented by my idol and watched by millions of people around the world. It was an epic experience for me, and it changed my life.

After the episode screened here, my career pretty much went through the roof. I got so many more bookings for private readings, and I also got asked to do a couple of charity events. Seeing me on TV even changed my dad's attitude towards me and all this 'clairvoyant rubbish', as he used to put it. It felt like for the first time in my life he accepted me for who I was.

And it also brought me to the attention of TV production company Ninox, who were making a programme called *Sensing Murder*. The rest, as they say, is history.

All of this came about because of Colin and the fact that he took a chance on me. We kept in contact, and I was really upset when he died in 2015 of lung cancer. He did so much to show the world what mediums can do – that we're not weirdos, but everyday people who just happen to have this ability to communicate with spirit and help loved ones deal with their grief.

Since he died Colin has continued to help me, often coming through in spirit to assist me with some of my readings. Colin was actually present when I met TJ in Japan, and she told me about how he had played a major part in her life.

Like me, TJ, a Londoner, started seeing spirit when she was young. After her grandfather died when she was about three or four, she would see him around the house all the time, often sitting in his favourite armchair. When she told her mother she could see Pops, her mum got angry and told her she wasn't to speak that way. I can relate to that kind of reaction from a parent.

TJ had lots of experiences with spirit growing up, including once hearing voices warning her not to accompany a so-called friend when the girl came to her house asking for help. (She ignored the voices, was lured out of her home and got beaten up by the girl and two others.)

But it wasn't until she was in her late twenties that she went to a psychic fair and saw a medium who told her she should join a mediumship circle, where people try to contact the spirit world. It was then that she started exploring her gift, and what she could do with it.

TJ began doing private readings and small public demonstrations, while going on courses and to workshops. There's far more access to that kind of development help in the UK than there is here. Some of the courses she did were taught by Tony Stockwell, another well-known medium. Through him she went along to an audition with the TV company that made *6ixth Sense with Colin Fry*, which was looking for a third medium to join Colin and Tony in a new TV series called *Psychic Private Eyes*. TJ impressed the producers with her abilities, and she made her TV debut in 2006.

TJ went on to become close to Colin, who invited her to tour with him. This was TJ's introduction to doing readings on stage in front of hundreds, and often thousands, of people. Colin became a mentor to her as well as a friend, and she toured the world with him, including coming to New Zealand in 2008. She was devastated when he died.

It was lovely to meet another medium who had known Colin and was grateful to him for the impact he had had on their life, like I was. We got talking about her trip to New Zealand with him, and then we came up with the idea of doing a tour around the country together, to honour Colin. We decided to call it *The Legacy Tour*, and planned to get to as many places as possible around New Zealand as we could.

I had never worked on stage with another medium before. I knew doing a 'tag-team' with TJ – having both of us on stage at the same time alternating readings, rather than doing a half of the show each – would probably be a challenge. But life is about trying new things, and I was up for it.

CHAPTER 10

Double act

'I woke up from my afternoon sleep with the song "Angie" playing in my head,' said TJ. 'I've got a lovely bloke with me, who came to me in my dream, and he's looking for Angie. Does that mean anything to anyone?'

We were a couple of nights into our *Legacy* tour around New Zealand in honour of Colin Fry, and TJ was kicking off the show in Papakura, South Auckland, with the first reading.

A woman put her hand up and said her name was Angie, and that song meant something to her.

'Is your husband in the other world?' asked TJ.

Angie shook her head.

'Sorry, you can't have this man,' replied TJ, to much laughter from the audience. 'As you're talking to me, he's looking at me like,

"No, what are you doing? That ain't mine." He's pretty yummy, but you can't have him.'

Another Angie put her hand up, and this time TJ established that yes, she did have the right person, so off she went on the reading. It was Angie's husband who had come through, and everything TJ said struck a chord.

'Was he a big guy? Would people describe him as a gentle giant?'

'Yes,' said Angie.

'He's not old – he was 40 to 45 when he passed.'

'He was 41.'

'Did he ride a motorbike? Not a sports bike; what I call one of those comfy bikes. I could hear a motorbike when I was in the dressing room.'

That didn't mean anything to start with, until Angie remembered they'd had their wedding photos taken on motorbikes, and yes, they were 'comfy bikes' – Harley Davidsons.

'There was no goodbye when he passed,' continued TJ. 'It's like he went to sleep and didn't wake up. I can't see anything else wrong with him. It was a peaceful passing.'

A tearful Angie acknowledged that that was what had happened.

Next TJ got the name Rodney, as in the character from the TV show *Only Fools and Horses*. It turned out that it didn't relate to a person, but to the Rodney Rams, a football club where Angie and her husband had hung out.

TJ knew that their footie strip was blue, and she also saw collection buckets, so she knew the club had raised money for the family. She came up with the name Catherine, which was his daughter's name, and she said he hadn't been on the other side for very long, probably less than a year.

'I think he must have missed Valentine's Day because he would have spoilt you; he had something planned. Did he pass close to February 14?' TJ asked.

'February 11,' Angie said. There was a gasp from the audience at that.

Every message TJ passed on resonated with Angie, although she didn't really respond when TJ said: 'He keeps showing me the sea and telling me I have to mention the ocean. It's important.'

They did have a boat, so it seemed to relate to that.

While this was going on, I was sitting on stage thinking, Wow, how amazing is this? TJ was totally nailing everything, and I wondered how I was going to follow that when it was my turn to read.

The thing was, I had also been able to connect with Angie's husband while TJ was doing the reading, and I could feel the love coming from him. It had me in tears. That man adored his wife.

I didn't want to gatecrash TJ's reading, but once she had finished I had to mention what Angie's husband had said to me.

'He talked about the tattoo that was significant,' I said to Angie. 'Has someone got a tattoo for him?'

'Yes,' said Angie. 'Me.'

There was a big 'ohhhh,' from the audience at that point.

'He's telling me that he loves it. Thumbs-up.'

'It's a fishing hook,' she explained.

'Huh, I'm a fisherman, and he didn't come to me in my dreams,' I joked.

I asked Angie if she minded explaining what the messages that TJ had been able to pass on meant to her. I wanted to highlight the fact that it didn't matter that TJ was from the other side of the world and had never heard of things like the Rodney Rams (neither had I, come to that), but it all comes down to spirit, who are just so cool when it comes to sharing relevant information.

'Everything was bang-on,' Angie said. 'My husband, Kirk, always sang the song "Angie" to me – really badly. He passed away in his sleep. It turns out he had heart disease, but there had been no sign of any illness. He just didn't wake up in the morning.'

Angie confirmed that they had a daughter, Catherine, and that the Rodney Rams had done a fundraiser to pay for Kirk's funeral.

She admitted she had been struggling with his death – it had only been a few months earlier – because she and Kirk were soulmates. I could certainly tell that.

'Wasn't TJ amazing?' I said. 'I might as well just go home!'

And as if all of that wasn't incredible enough, TJ added, 'All I could hear when I did that reading was "I love the ocean, I love the ocean".'

'We always went fishing together,' explained Angie. 'He'd be on the boat fishing and I'd be paddle-boarding and diving and snorkelling. That was our happy place, out on the water.'

And then TJ said, 'Does "ocean" mean something else to you, though? He's saying to me, "No, that's not right." There's something else about the ocean that is important.'

'Oh,' said Angie. 'We've got a daughter called Ocean.'

Well.

The place exploded.

How incredible was that? It totally blew me and everyone else in the theatre away.

Despite all my good-natured grumbling about going home and leaving the rest of the show up to TJ because that was such an epic reading, I was so happy to hear her nail it like that. I wanted people to understand it wasn't a competition between us, we weren't trying to prove one of us got better information than the other from spirit.

What it was about was spirit, and how amazing they are. It doesn't matter whether you're from Ngaruawahia, London or Timbuktu, when spirit come through and start sharing with you, it can be incredible.

The TJ and KC show

To be honest, I have never had a lot to do with other mediums. Some of them are a little bit – how do I put this nicely? – strange. I've always preferred to do my thing on my own, and I've never felt the need to hang out with a bunch of others who talk with dead people and compare notes.

But from the moment I met TJ there was an instant rapport, and for the first time ever I thought about sharing a stage with someone else. Next thing I knew, the New Zealand tour was being planned, and tickets were being sold. TJ and her partner and manager, Stu, arrived in June 2019 and, after a few days of getting over the jetlag and hanging out with me up in the Bay of Islands, we hit the road. We did 16 shows in 19 days, which was probably a little bit ambitious, but TJ had limited time, so we just needed to get on with it.

We had only a couple of days when we didn't do shows, and they were filled with either doing workshops or flying around the country. We did just three flights, the rest of the time we drove; and all I can say is thank goodness for Stu. He ended up doing all of the driving, and as a result we nicknamed him Parker, after the chauffeur in the TV series *Thunderbirds*. He was a legend.

We'd get up in the morning having done a show the night before and hit the road, with Stu behind the wheel and me in the front seat next to him. TJ would sit in the back seat, surrounded by bags and boxes of her books, which she had carted all the way over here to sell at shows, and she'd usually be reading. I don't know how she managed to do that in the back of the car.

We'd arrive in the next town, check into our motel, and have a quick nana nap before heading for the venue to prepare for the show. Along the way I did get to show TJ and Stu a little bit of the country – we even got to Bluff – but there wasn't a lot of time for the touristy stuff.

We had one pretty hairy day when bad weather closed the airport at Tauranga, meaning we had to drive from there to Palmerston North for the next show. It was a six-and-a-half-hour trip, but Parker got us there in one piece an hour and a half before the show started.

Stu's not a big bloke, but he was more than worth his weight in gold, not only for the driving he did, but also because he was so helpful during the shows, taking tickets, handing out the microphone to the people getting a reading, and generally being Mr Helpful.

I didn't take a member of my crew on the road with me, but some of the lovely ladies from around the country who help out whenever I am in their neck of the woods stepped up and assisted us, too, which was great.

I have to admit, being on stage with another medium and working in tandem did take a bit of getting used to. There were some teething problems with sound at a couple of venues, which meant neither of us could hear what the other was saying. And there were times when it got quite confusing with spirit all over the place. Eventually I realised the best thing to do was to turn my microphone off when I wasn't speaking, and that shut spirit down. It also stopped me from wanting to chip in with what I was getting from spirit while TJ was reading. I didn't want to interfere and jump in over the top of her.

There were a couple of times, though, when I did connect with the same spirit as TJ, and I just had to say something. Like with Angie, the lady whose husband showed me the tattoo she'd had done for him.

Another time a young guy who had been killed in an accident came through for TJ, and while she was talking to his family, he turned to me and went, 'Check this out, man! Look at me, I'm rolling a joint.' He was like a naughty teenager.

While TJ was being all serious with the family – she couldn't see what he was doing – I was sitting there giggling. He was a real character, that guy.

When TJ finished her reading and sat down, I flicked my microphone on and asked if she minded me adding to what she had said.

'While you were reading, I had him showing me that he was trying to roll a joint,' I said. I figured I had been shown this for a reason, so I might as well mention it.

His family cracked up at that. 'That would be right,' said his brother.

He had been a bit of a rat-bag when it came to the weed while he was on this side of life, and showing me that was a way of confirming that, yes, it was him.

He said to me, 'This is what I used to be like; I'm not doing it now, but this will convince my family that it really is me.'

His family seemed to appreciate that, and it lightened the air after what had been a pretty emotional reading with TJ.

A couple of times we did actually read the same person at the same time, which was pretty phenomenal. It didn't happen very often, but it was really amazing when it did.

Different strokes for different folks

TJ and I have really different ways of working. If you've been to one of my shows, you'll know that I will start chatting to spirit before I work out who they are there for.

I ask them to be really direct when it comes to finding the person they need to connect with. Occasionally I can pick out their family member because they will have a kind of glow about them, and I will know, Right, that is where I am meant to be.

But generally when I start communicating with spirit they'll say

'Bro, my brother's out there', so I'll say 'Who is he?' Sometimes a description is enough to help me find the person.

The guy in spirit might say 'He's the one in the black hat with the moustache and glasses', and immediately I'll be able to spot his brother and start the reading. But sometimes it is a little more complicated. People can be harder to find if spirit aren't great on descriptions. Telling me 'The lady with the white hair' isn't going to be helpful at most of my shows.

So I will tell spirit to go find the person and tap them on the shoulder, and if you watch me, I seem to be following someone as they move through the audience. In fact, I am following spirit.

Then the reading will begin, and I'll start sorting out the information that is being thrown at me. I'll often be shown other family members who have passed over, so I will say to the guy I'm reading for: 'As well as your brother, have both your parents also passed over? Is there a child who died? I can see them, too. And I've got your nana here, she's in the corner knitting.'

Often I get a whole whānau coming through – it's like there is a mini-bus full of spirit people just waiting to come and say hi.

Sometimes I get names, sometimes I don't. If a woman comes through for her daughter, she's most likely going to describe herself as Mum and not give her first name. After all, when she was on this side that's how her daughter knew her.

There are times when I will get the first initial of a name, but spirit are more likely to give me information about things they did while they were here that the person getting a reading can relate to, rather than names or physical descriptions.

TJ, meanwhile, starts off by describing the person in spirit who has come through to her, and then asks the audience if anyone can relate to what she's saying. She might say: 'I've got a lady with curly hair, she's wearing a pinny and she loves to cook. She's talking about a man called Sidney and his wife, Annette.'

And then it turns out there's a guy in the audience called Sidney, and sitting next to him is his wife, Annette, and Sidney's mum was an excellent cook.

TJ is phenomenal when it comes to names – it is freakish how often she gets those right. She will often start hearing or seeing stuff before the show starts, and, in a lot of cases, songs will give her a clue to who she should be reading for – like the Rolling Stones song "Angie".

Before a show I will also sometimes get clues about the readings that are coming up. I've had situations where I've arrived at a theatre and been walking around beforehand, doing my karakia or blessing, and I've smelled smoke or heard a helicopter. Sure enough, my readings those nights included a woman who died in a fire and a man killed in a helicopter crash.

TJ tends to get just one person coming through per reading, so it is less chaotic than when I get my busloads of people.

So we work quite differently, but at the end of the day we get the same result. We get to pass on messages from spirit to their loved ones, and hopefully help those people who get readings – and everyone else in the audience – to understand that when we die we don't stop existing, we just go to another place.

Next stop, UK!

The Legacy Tour with TJ was hard work and tiring, but it was also a lot of fun and we were able to share some really amazing messages. It's not always easy to make yourself understood when you are in another country (remember my Japanese experience!) and even when you speak the same language there are often phrases they use in the UK that don't mean anything to us here, and vice versa. But TJ was a quick learner and she soon picked up many of our

Kiwi-isms, like jandals and lollies. She was even saying 'Kia ora' to the audiences after a few days.

She has a great way with people, she's very bubbly, warm and outgoing, and she was able to bring comfort to so many audience members she read for. I know she's gained a huge number of Kiwi fans following her time here. We've now planned for me to go to the UK to join her on a tour there, and I can't wait.

It's been such a pleasure to work with TJ and to get to know her and Stu. Here's to more collaboration in the future.

I think we did Colin proud.

TJ says

I clicked with Kelvin from the moment we met. He feels like a male version of me, a twin brother who had been missing. Our upbringing and our experiences with spirit and family members who have passed are very similar. Plus we have silly little things in common that have nothing to do with mediumship. When we were at Kelvin's before starting the tour he cooked us dinner, and when pudding was served Kelvin and I both went to the drawer to get out a little spoon. We both like to eat pudding with a teaspoon. Weird!

I also liked the fact that he was very respectful of Stu. A lot of people dismiss Stu because they want to get to me, but Kelvin did the opposite: he was very thoughtful towards Stu.

When we met in Japan I had already been considering coming to New Zealand, and I was sitting there thinking, Oh, it would be lovely to work with Kelvin. Clearly he was thinking the same thing, because in the end he said, 'Would you like to come and tour with me in New Zealand?' I said I would love to.

We both had this history with Colin, and he was present when we were talking about doing a tour, so the obvious thing to do was to make it in honour of him. Nobody else has ever done that, yet Colin is the person who paved the way for so many mediums to do what they are doing now.

In the UK we'd had famous mediums who did the big theatres, like Doris Stokes, but nobody had done a TV programme showing how a medium worked. It gave people an idea of what we are about and showed that we're not spooky or scary. Colin was just this nice guy standing there talking to people's relatives.

There was still some controversy around what he did, but if he hadn't stepped out and put his head above the parapet Kelvin and I wouldn't be doing what we do. Colin was a great ambassador for spirit, and he opened so many doors.

He also had a great personality and was so much fun, which you didn't always see on his TV show. From the moment Colin and I met it was as if we had known each other all of our lives. He'd start a sentence and I would finish it.

I first met Colin when I landed the job on the TV series *Psychic Private Eyes*. At the audition I was given envelopes that contained information about a murder victim whose killer hadn't been caught at that stage. As I put my hand on the envelope, the girl who had been killed was standing at the end of the table. I could smell onions, as if I was in a pub kitchen, and the girl, whose name was Sally Anne, kept saying 'Marks all over me, marks all over me'. They later caught the guy who did it – his name was Mark and he was a pub chef.

When Colin said to me one day, 'You're coming on tour with me,' I said, 'No way, you're crazy!' At that stage I was doing private readings and teaching as well as TV, but I didn't get up on stage. That didn't matter to Colin, he just dragged me along with him and that was that.

As well as touring around the UK, we went to Norway, America and New Zealand together. I have been doing stage shows on my own now for the past 10 years, so it was good to work with someone else again. I didn't realise that Kelvin had never worked with anyone before, so it is a big deal that he trusted me to share his stage, and his fans. I was very conscious that I didn't want to let Kelvin down in any way; by inviting me along he was saying to his audiences: 'She's a good medium, you've got to watch her.'

We do work very differently. I make a connection, get to know who I am talking with and get the feeling of them, and then they show me who I am going to. I watch how Kelvin works and think, Wow, I don't know how you do it. He says he thinks the same thing about me. I think it is beautiful for the audience to see the two of us working in opposite ways but achieving the same thing – bringing forward spirit, and the love they have for the person we are reading.

When Kelvin was reading, I switched off. I didn't want to be linking into him, as that would take away his energy. Most of the time I sat patiently, and spirit would often start showing themselves to me while I was waiting. They might start singing a song to me, or I would be able to see them when I looked at the wall in the theatre.

We did have one experience where things got a bit dramatic with Kelvin's reading, and when I started mine the first two names I got were actually connected with the reading he had just done. Another time we got a double link: I connected with the dad, and he connected with the child.

One thing I have noticed in New Zealand is that you get a lot more readings involving suicide than we do in the UK. I might do three a month here, but in New Zealand it seemed like there was one at nearly every show we did. It's a bit like Japan in that respect – I do a lot more readings there with people who have taken their lives. They are very sad, but the beauty of our work is that we can show their families that they are not in a dark place, they are in the arms of people who love them.

I did a lovely reading for a young man called Jamie, when his friend who had committed suicide came through. He basically gave Jamie a kick up the bum about getting his life sorted. He also gave Jamie a message to give to his dad.

I asked Jamie to keep in touch with me and let me know how he got on, and I was pleased to hear back from him. He told me he was going to rehab, which was great news. He said he'd also been in touch with his friend's dad, who'd always blamed himself for his son's death, and the dad was finally able to let that go.

I know Kelvin does a lot of suicide readings, and he handles them so well. I watch the people he's talking to in the audience and I can see their energy changing. I can see the weight lifted from their shoulders, and I think, Yes, this is why we do this.

He's got such a big following in New Zealand, and it is interesting to see the way people respond to him in public. They all want to say hello. Everyone seems to know who he is, whereas in England, even when I would be out in public with Colin at the time we were both appearing on TV, not everyone would know who we were.

I think the reason people respond to Kelvin is because he keeps it real. He is on stage being himself. And he loves what he does. When I am working with him on stage I can feel his passion. It's like when a child gets excited about something – they just light up. When spirit are talking to Kelvin, he really comes alive.

You can tell that he really cares by the way he interacts with people. Unfortunately, with a lot of mediums it is all about them – 'Aren't I good? Aren't I clever?' Kelvin's not like that, he's very humble. This is not about him being a showman. He just loves being able to help people, same as me. I'm looking forward to working with him again.

BACK ON HOME SOIL

CHAPTER 11

Time to pay it forward

I'd like to share a story with you. Way back in 1978, when I was just a nipper, over in America a woman called Catherine Ryan Hyde got herself into a spot of bother late one night. She was driving through a dodgy part of Los Angeles when her ancient old Datsun stalled as she came to a stop at the end of a freeway off-ramp. To her horror, smoke then started curling out of the dashboard.

Catherine was stuck between a rock and a hard place: if she stayed where she was, she could be risking her life if the car burst into flames; but if she got out of the car she could also be putting her safety on the line, because she was in a seriously dangerous part of town that she normally drove through with her doors locked. I've been to some of those parts of LA and I don't blame her for not wanting to get out of her car, even if it was on fire. I'd think twice.

Catherine had to make a decision, and she had to do it fast. The car was now properly on fire, so she jumped out. And then she spotted two men running towards her, one of them carrying a blanket. She had visions of being wrapped up in the blanket and abducted, and thought she was about to experience the last moments of her life.

But to her huge relief, the two strangers ran past her. One reached into her car and popped the bonnet – or the hood, as they say in the US – while the other one opened it and leaned over the engine, smothering the flames with the blanket. If it hadn't been for them, the car could have exploded.

In the meantime, somebody else had called the fire brigade, which arrived soon afterwards, and in the chaos that ensued Catherine didn't get a chance to speak to the men who had come to her rescue. When she looked for them to say thank you, they had gone.

So why am I telling you this? Well, it really troubled Catherine that she hadn't been able to pay those two men back for what they had done. And then one day she came up with an idea. Since she couldn't pay the favour back to those men, why not pay it *forward* to someone else? She began looking for people she could help, such as stranded motorists who needed a ride. When she was asked why she was helping complete strangers, she explained the pay-it-forward concept. When the people she helped asked if they could pay her back, she told them to pay it forward.

Catherine's idea about helping others became well known around the world thanks to the fact that she's a writer. Twenty years after the original incident, she wrote a novel called *Pay It Forward*, about a 12-year-old boy whose teacher assigns the class to come up with a plan that can change the world for better. He devises the pay-it-forward concept.

The following year the book was made into a movie starring Kevin Spacey, Helen Hunt and Haley Joel Osment (the kid from *The Sixth Sense*), and it became a huge hit. Better yet, the concept of paying it forward became a major global movement. While the idea behind pay it forward had been mentioned in earlier literature, the concept didn't really grab people's attention until after the movie came out. It has certainly taken off in a huge way since, from people incorporating the idea into their daily lives with small gestures, through to foundations being set up to encourage us to do good things for others on a grand scale.

It is a concept that has changed the world, and it's fascinating to know that the whole pay-it-forward movement might not have happened if those two anonymous men – who have never been found – hadn't helped Catherine Ryan Hyde that day, and then left without waiting to be thanked.

I heard this story from my ghostwriter Donna. In her other life Donna is a journalist, and she got to meet and interview Catherine, which she says was a highlight of her career. It was really cool to learn how all of this came about, particularly because the pay-it-forward concept is something I have tried to put into practice throughout my life. I have learned on my spiritual journey that one of the main reasons we are here is to help others. It may not be as major as saving someone's life by putting out a fire in their car, but even thoughtful little gestures can make a world of difference to someone. I think the idea of doing random acts of kindness for strangers is really important, because it restores our faith in humanity. In a world where sadly there are a lot of horrible people doing terrible things to others, a thoughtful gesture is a reminder that there are good people out there, too.

And while it is wonderful to do nice things for strangers, it is also important to be kind to those people around you. I try to make a habit of helping my mates when I can. Even many years ago, when

I had no money and was living in my van, I would do little things for my friends if I could. When I started earning a decent living, I was able to step it up and assist in other ways, like helping a mate with their mortgage payment if they were struggling that month, or handing over my bank-card to pay for their groceries. Why wouldn't you do that if you could?

But it's not all about money. A while back I realised that a couple of my friends were really stressed, because people were coming to stay at their home and they were so busy working that they hadn't had time to get the place cleaned up. So I said to Javan, 'Let's go around there and see what we can do.'

We cruised around, let ourselves in (they don't lock their place) and, to be honest, it was worse than we thought. The kitchen looked like a bomb had gone off, and their chickens had got out of their pen and made a terrible mess of the deck. So I got stuck into the waterblasting while Javan tackled the kitchen. He did the dishes, scrubbed the surfaces, cleaned the cupboards, emptied the rubbish and washed the floor. Then he got out the vacuum cleaner and vacuumed the lounge. It took a couple of hours of our time, but it lifted a huge amount of stress from our mates. And knowing we had been able to do that for them felt choice.

I have been lucky enough to have been on the receiving end of thoughtful acts myself, so I know what a difference it can make. I've come home after doing shows around the country feeling exhausted and utterly drained, and driven up my road thinking, Oh crap, the lawns are going to be like a jungle. Then I've pulled into my drive only to see that some wonderful soul has mowed my grass for me. Over the years my mates have weeded my garden, cleaned out my spouting and re-stained my entire deck. I've come home to find the housework done and a freezer full of crayfish. Some of their kind deeds have been a response to things I have done for them – for example, I've had a trailer-load of firewood delivered as a thank-you from a friend I took out on my boat. But they have also helped me out because they've thought, Oh KC will be shattered after doing all these shows; let's do his garden so he can have a rest when he gets home. And can I just say, they do a much better job of my garden than me – my idea of gardening is to spray Roundup over everything. And then I wonder why so many of my plants die.

A little bit of kindness goes a long way, and if we all made the effort to do something thoughtful for others it would definitely help to make up for some of the shitty stuff that goes on in this world.

Doing my bit

If you follow me on Facebook, you may have noticed over the past few years that by the end of every November it looks as though there's a dead cat embedded in my top lip. That is because I have been a very keen supporter of Movember – which raises money for, and awareness of, men's health – and I have attempted to grow the requisite moustache for the event. Facial hair is not my friend, and every year I have been hanging out for 1 December, when I can shave off that horrible itchy growth.

I have also got together with my mates to do fishing competitions for Movember – our team name was the MoFoBroz – and over the years, we raised around $18,000 in one month, one year even becoming the most successful Movember fundraising team.

Unlike the mo-growing, the fishing is a lot of fun, but we never forget that it is for a serious cause. I became involved not only to raise funds, but also to get men talking about their health. We blokes are terrible at taking action when it comes to things going wrong in our body. I know a lot of guys think they have to be staunch and just put up with health problems, but that's not being tough, it's being stupid. It is not weak to seek help, it is smart, and you could save your life if you go to the doctor sooner rather than later.

So anything I can do to encourage men to change this potentially dangerous way of thinking and be proactive about their health is important to me. As you'll know, having a public profile and being a 'celebrity' of sorts, thanks to being on TV, is not something I particularly enjoy. But if I can use the fact that quite a few people know who I am to do something useful, then I will.

I have supported numerous other charities over the years, too, some publicly and others by doing things behind the scenes. In 2018, after having a pretty epic year – which kicked off in February with finding Raymond Stirling – I decided I wanted to do something major to help out a deserving organisation. My team and I came up with the idea of a *Pay It Forward* show, in which we would promote a worthwhile charity and donate money from events like a silent auction.

The first idea that came to my mind was to find an organisation supporting people affected by dementia. Giving money to them would be a way of honouring Curly, who had dementia. (At that stage, I hadn't found John, who also had the disease.) It would also be a way of supporting a charity that does a great job of helping people with this devastating condition. Over 60,000 Kiwis have some form of dementia, and it not only turns their lives upside down, it also takes a huge toll on those who end up caring for them.

I was very excited about the prospect of being able to give money to this cause, and my team approached an organisation about our idea of a *Pay It Forward* show. So when we got an email back saying no thanks, we don't want to accept money from you, I was upset and felt like I had been kicked in the guts. I remember sitting outside on my deck with my head in my hands feeling utterly heartbroken. I only wanted to help, but, because I am a medium, my help was not wanted. Taking money from a guy who talks with dead people was not acceptable.

I sat there for a while thinking, What is the point in me even doing what I do? How can people think I am the lowest of the low, simply because I try to help people who are grieving and missing their loved ones? Why do I bother if this is what people think of me? I have been rejected a lot in my life, but that one really ripped. But then I realised I had to pull myself together and not let the response of one organisation knock me down. I was helped in this by my team member Gemma, who tells it like it is, when she said to me, 'Look, KC, why don't you just pull your head out of your backside, get over it and find a charity that will accept your support wholeheartedly? In fact, have you thought about Mike King's I Am Hope charity? Why don't we see if he's interested?'

As soon as Gemma mentioned Mike's name I felt this surge of positivity. Of all the organisations out there doing their best to help Kiwis (and there are a hell of a lot of them), Mike's suicide prevention and mental health charity was a great fit with what I do. Through my work, I have met numerous people whose lives have been devastated by the suicide of a loved one. And I've also had lots of interactions with those in spirit who have taken their own lives. Plus, I've lost people I care about to suicide and I know the toll it can take.

What Mike does is amazing, and I felt that it would be a privilege to do my bit to support him. I really hoped he would be open to the idea of taking money from someone who talks to dead people. If he'd said no I'd have been gutted.

An outstanding human being

Every now and then, someone comes along who sticks their neck out for a cause they are passionate about, walks the talk and becomes a true hero. And it is not always who you expect it to be.

Who'd have thought, when we were watching Mike King on TV all those years ago, that this stand-up comedian who had us in fits of laughter would end up tackling the very serious subject of mental health and suicide prevention? It turns out he's had his own issues with depression and addiction, and so in 2009 he founded *The Nutters Club*, which started out as a Facebook page and went on to become a radio and TV show that has helped tens of thousands of Kiwis affected by mental illness to live more peacefully with themselves. He also encourages people to call in and talk about their experiences, which I think is a brilliant thing to do. It helps to remove some of the stigma around mental illness, and lets people know they are not alone.

In 2012 he founded the Key To Life Charitable Trust, which in turn created the I Am Hope movement. Not only does Mike travel up and down the country, visiting schools to talk about suicide prevention and share the message that there is always hope, but he is also raising money to pay for counselling for kids, so they can get the support they need, when they need it most.

Mike has taken a lot on his shoulders to do this, and he really deserved to be named New Zealander of the Year in 2019. He is an outstanding human being with a big heart, and I really can't praise him enough. He is making a huge difference.

He's also very honest and straight-up, and I knew there would be no messing around with him. If he didn't want me to help, he would tell me. Thankfully, he was stoked with the offer and said yes please.

Once we got the go-ahead from Mike and his team, we set about organising the *Pay It Forward* show. This was not simply a case of me rocking up to the venue – in this case a school in Auckland – and getting on stage and having a chat with spirit. It was a massive undertaking that involved lots of different fundraising events, including an online auction that people unable to attend the show could still take part in. Because it was being held close to Christmas, we had a remembrance Christmas tree where you could buy a star in memory of a loved one, and I would choose a star from the tree and do a reading for the person who had bought it. In the lobby, we also had a marketplace with numerous stalls.

None of this would have happened if it wasn't for Gemma. She oversaw everything, from organising the items to be donated for the auction right through to sending them out afterwards, which was a mammoth undertaking. She spent hours and hours on Facebook, publicising the event, letting people know what was on offer and answering hundreds of questions. In a particularly thoughtful touch, she enlisted the help of her musician friend Brad Stent to write a song with her, which they recorded. (She's a very talented singer.) The song was played along with a slideshow of photos of people who have lost their lives to suicide, which had been sent in to Gemma via Facebook. It really hit home, seeing those photos and knowing that all of those people are no longer with us.

The song is so poignant and beautiful, and is the perfect accompaniment to the slideshow – search up 'A Million Reasons: Suicide Awareness and Prevention Tribute' on YouTube and you'll see what I mean. Have some tissues handy when you do, though.

Organising everything was a full-time job, but Gemma did it all on a voluntary basis. She's a gem, our Gemma.

Gemma says

The *Pay It Forward* show was a huge job, but it was really good to be able to help Mike King – the man is a legend and he single-handedly saves lives. I knew he would be grateful because he relies so much on donations.

And suicide prevention and awareness was a really fitting

subject for Kelvin to be involved with because it comes up so much in his work. He does so many readings at his shows that relate to suicide – and when I am there I often end up talking to the people who have lost someone to suicide, and it is so sad.

I oversee Kelvin's Facebook page, and what's even harder is the number of messages there from people reaching out for help after someone close to them has died from suicide. I would say we get one at least every two or three days, and I think we get more messages about suicide than anything else, including losing people to cancer. We really have a massive problem in New Zealand.

Kelvin and I have both lost loved ones to suicide, so we understand what it is like to lose someone this way. It usually comes out of nowhere and is such a huge shock. It is very cool when Kelvin is able to help someone who is going through this.

It is so important to raise awareness, and we thought that if we could do this, as well as raise money and help people with their grief, then it would be a win-win-win situation.

I really wanted to have a song especially for the show – I think music is the key to the soul and definitely helps you through the hard times. However, I couldn't find anything that said what I wanted to say, so I went to my friend Brad, who is an amazing musician and songwriter, and we worked on the lyrics together and he composed the music. He also put together the slideshow. The chorus is a reminder that there are a million reasons for holding on and continuing to live, no matter what we are feeling. I hope hearing that helps someone.

Tears and laughter

We did a buy-one-get-one-free ticket offer for the *Pay It Forward* show, and the venue was packed. I have to admit that by the time the show rolled around, I was pretty exhausted. It was the last show of the year and I was ready for a break.

Every show I do is draining – it takes a lot of effort and energy for me to talk to spirit and understand the messages I am getting back. And if I am dealing with really emotional stuff, then that tends to take a toll on me, too.

The *Pay It Forward* show was particularly emotional, especially after Mike got on stage first and did a bit of a korero (talk) about his charity and what he was trying to achieve. I was just about in tears before I even got on the stage.

I didn't actually do a suicide reading that night, but there were tears shed over quite a few readings. There was a man in spirit who apologised to his granddaughter for pain he'd inflicted on the family, and another woman who came through for a dear friend who'd really been struggling without her. I could feel their anguish.

There was some laughter, too. A guy who had died tragically came through for a lady I was reading for, and talked about how he joined her and her husband when they went out on their boat fishing. 'Oh, the things you two get up to on that boat!' I said, relaying the message I was getting from spirit. The poor woman went bright red. I'd obviously struck a chord there.

I also ended up doing a reading for Mike King's wife, Jo. Her mum turned up right at the beginning of the show, but I was reluctant to talk to her because I thought people might think it was a set-up, and I was reading for someone I know. As it was I didn't actually know Jo, but I held off connecting with her mum until at the start of the second half it got to the point where I had to say something because Jo's mum just wasn't going to go away.

'She really wants me to tell you that she's dancing again, so don't worry,' I told Jo. 'And she says, "I don't look like I did before I left."' By the look on Jo's face, I think hearing that gave her a lot of comfort.

At one stage during the reading Mike chipped in: 'Just so everyone knows, I didn't say anything to Kelvin'.

Jo's mum told her not to despair over her loss; she was still there watching over her and the family. I had to quickly add, 'It's all right, Mike, she's not watching you in the shower – you're safe.'

She also wanted to let Jo know that she would be able to get through anything that cropped up, and that she had loved her funeral. 'Everything was perfect – you did me proud.'

At one point I was seeing an image from an old TV ad from many years ago; I didn't quite understand why, but I just went with it. 'Your mum wants to throw Jaffas down the aisle,' I said, remembering the commercial in which someone spills a packet of the lollies in a cinema.

'She used to be an usherette at a movie theatre,' Jo said.

It turned out to be a lovely reading, and, as I told Jo, it was a real privilege for me to connect with her mum. But the best part was that I was able to share some really special information: 'She had her struggles in life, but she came through them, and now she's got her wings. Your mum's an angel.'

I'm glad I was able to give that message to Jo. All in all, it turned out to be a pretty amazing evening, and in the end we raised $14,600. I was stoked to be able to give that to Mike to help him continue to do the incredible job he does of saving lives. It was an absolute honour to be able to support his work, and anytime he needs anything from me, I'll be there.

CHAPTER 12

Home, sweet home

It's an absolutely magic moment, and it gets to me every single time. Whenever I'm flying back to New Zealand after being overseas and I catch my first glimpse of home as the plane descends through the clouds, I feel a ripple of emotion at the sight of our beautiful green land and the white-topped waves rushing towards it. There's often a lump in my throat and a tear in my eye as I look out the window and think, 'Thank God I'm home'.

Getting to travel overseas is one of the perks of my job, and I feel so lucky to get the chance to go to places like the United States and Japan. But nothing beats coming home. It's not just that I get to be in the same country as my kids and everyone else important to me. Or that New Zealand feels so much safer – and saner – than many of the places where I've been working. Yes, I know we have crime in this country and there are a lot of things we need to work on, but when you've been dealing with cases involving serial killers and sex trafficking New Zealand feels so much less scary.

It also feels so much more spiritual than many other countries, and I put that down to our Māori culture, which is founded on strong spiritual beliefs. Māori have huge respect for Nature, for the land and ocean, for their tūpuna (ancestors), for their gods and for spirit. The more I learn about the Māori culture – and I have only scratched the surface – the more I am in awe of their traditional beliefs. It is all about respect, and I think that is so vital. A lot of the issues in the world today are due to a lack of respect. We haven't respected our planet, and look at our problems with climate change. We haven't respected each other and the differences we have, which is why there is so much conflict around the world.

I love the way Māori culture has great respect for wairua (spirit). Some of my earliest encounters with spirit as a child were with Māori warriors who used to come out of the bush behind our house and stand outside my window, speaking to me in Māori. I was four when this started, and they scared the living daylights out of me. It wasn't until my pop, Monty Haack, died four years later and then came to me in spirit that I learned from him that they were warriors who had been killed in fighting on the land surrounding our home in Rotongaro, which had essentially been a battlefield back in the day. When he came to me, Pop said, 'These fellas are all right.' They stopped troubling me after that.

But it wasn't until I was in my twenties, and a lot more spiritually developed after finally accepting my path in life, that I understood that they were lost souls. Because of the way they had died, they had been unable to cross through to the light and were trapped. On a visit back to Rotongaro I stood opposite the bush and I called them into the light, so they could cross over. It was a beautiful moment.

HOME, SWEET HOME

A special place

Most Kiwis understand the significance of Cape Reinga to the Māori people. Located at the northern tip of the North Island, the cape is also known as Te Rerenga Wairua or the leaping-off place of the spirits. It is where spirit leave the land of Aotearoa to start their journey back to their homeland of Hawaiiki – the mythical spiritual home of the Māori people. The cape is an incredibly sacred place, and as you look down from the cliffs you can see where the Tasman Sea to the west merges with the Pacific Ocean to the east.

Māori believe that when you die your spirit goes on a hīkoi, or journey, to Cape Reinga, and when the moon and tides are right your spirit crosses into the next world by climbing down the roots of the 800-year-old pohutukawa tree living there.

Cape Reinga is a very special place, and, being only a couple of hours from where I live in the Bay of Islands, I get a lot of visitors who say, 'Oh, since we're this far north, can we go up to Cape Reinga?' Yet while I genuinely love the place, to be honest I have been there so many times, and I've got to the stage where I'm a bit over it. And another major problem I have whenever I go there is that I get inundated with spirit. As I walk along the path to the Cape Reinga lighthouse, I get slammed by spirit on their way to jump off and head into the next world. There are so many of them I can feel them pushing past me. I can also feel the sadness of these spirit people that they are leaving behind their loved ones. There's a kind of heaviness associated with the place.

I've noticed when I am with friends or guests who are also sensitive to spirit that they feel it, too. While most people around us are oblivious – all these tourists going click, click, click with their cameras and walking through the middle of a bunch of spirit people – there are others who go all quiet and next thing you know they're saying, 'Why am I crying?'

I know why. It's because there is a kuia standing behind them saying 'I didn't get to say goodbye to my whānau and now I have to go.' She's feeling sad, so anyone who can tune into spirit picks up on it. And there's not just one person in spirit there doing this, there are dozens of them. When you can pick up on them like I can, it gets pretty intense.

Last summer, for the first time I went to Cape Reinga on my boat. It was a completely different experience to going there by land, and one that will stay with me for a long time. My good friend Matua Tata – otherwise known as Uncle – had come up from Rotorua to stay with me, and I thought it would be nice to take him out on the boat for his seventy-fifth birthday. (He cracks me up. When I first got a bigger boat and said we could do more adventurous trips, he said, 'No thanks, you won't get me on that boat.' Then he tried it and now I can't get him off!)

My tā moko (tattoo) artist Paitangi came with us on the trip last summer. Although we had planned to spend only a few days away, we were having such a good time that nobody wanted to go home. The days were spent fishing and diving, and hanging out on the boat, playing cards and relaxing. On Uncle's actual birthday we had an amazing feed of crayfish, scallops, oysters, mussels, snapper, kina and terakihi. It was spectacular.

When we got to beautiful Cape Karikari, I started thinking about whether it would be possible to keep heading north to Cape Reinga. I looked at how much fuel we had, checked out the weather patterns, and realised it was going to be possible. I thought, Sweet, let's do this.

I didn't tell Uncle where we were headed, and when we got to Spirits Bay, just south of Cape Reinga, I anchored up for the day.

'This is nice. Where are we?' Uncle asked.

'Um, I'm not sure,' I said. Of course I knew exactly where we were, but I wasn't telling him that.

HOME, SWEET HOME

Spirits Bay has to be one of the most beautiful places in New Zealand, and Uncle, who is very sensitive spiritually, immediately realised it was a special place.

'This feels really cool,' he told me.

The next morning I got up early, pulled up the anchor and headed for Cape Reinga. When I got close, I went and woke Uncle. 'Come up, there's something you need to see,' I told him.

The sun was rising, and it was the most spectacular sight. As you come out of Spirits Bay, heading to the cape, the cliffs are dotted with caves.

'Look, my friend, here are the caves of your ancestors,' I told Uncle. It was emotional for all of us.

Just being in such a sacred place was sending chills through Uncle, Paitangi and me. As we got closer to Cape Reinga, Pai stood at the front of the boat and did a karanga (the traditional Māori call of acknowledgement) to pay her respects to her ancestors. It made all the hair on my skin stand on end. The three of us are all spiritual people and we felt incredibly moved.

Later, as we sat on the edge of the boat watching the two oceans crash together, I said to Uncle and Pai: 'Have you guys noticed how peaceful it is?'

They both had, and for me it was a hugely different experience to when I am on the land at Cape Reinga and surrounded by spirit.

'I'm not being slammed by spirit because they're not here anymore – they've crossed over,' I told them.

The sense of serenity we all felt was off the charts. We said our karakia and went to have a look at the point where the two oceans come crashing together, which is amazing. As we were cruising back, I decided it might be good to stop and try a spot of fishing. At that point we were pretty much straight under the lighthouse, where the water is around 75 metres deep, which is not very deep. I put four lures out, and all of a sudden four marlin jumped on – boom,

boom, boom, boom! There were more marlin surrounding the boat, going crazy: it was just mind-blowing.

Seeing a marlin coming up past the bow of your boat like a dolphin, and then his mates popping up beside him, is all I need from life! Seeing so many like that is called a pack attack, and on the east coast it is unusual – you normally don't get any more than two or three. We had eight fish fighting over the lures, and it was as if Nature was saying to us, 'You've paid your respects, now here's our gift.'

Three of the marlin dropped off the lure and then one busted off, taking my lure with it. So we threw out bait, and Paitangi caught a little marlin – her first. We tagged it, took some photos, gave it a cuddle and sent it on its way. There is no point in keeping something you are not planning on eating. We had plenty of kai, so we sent it back to the ocean.

The experiences we had that day were amazing, and it was extra special because I got to share them with two very spiritual people. For as long as I live I will never forget that incredible sense of pure peace, and then the marlin going crazy. I can't imagine experiencing something like that anywhere else than New Zealand.

A spiritual search

Hearing a karanga is an awesome experience. Like a haka, it is a huge mark of respect and I always get goosebumps. When it comes from someone like Paitangi, who is a particularly strong and spiritual person, it resonates even more. I've heard her do it on several other occasions apart from that time at Cape Reinga, including on a road trip up north with friends one summer, and every time I am blown away.

For years Uncle had been saying to me: 'KC, we need to find

the grave of my kuia, it's really important.' Unfortunately, he didn't know where his grandmother was buried, though, so we started off looking around Kaeo, which is where he thought she might be, but we had no luck. And every time we've gone up north we've tried to find her.

Then earlier this year a group of us went on a road trip up to the Waipoua Forest to see Tāne Mahuta, New Zealand's largest known kauri tree. Named after the god of the trees and birds, Tāne is incredibly majestic, but in recent years has been threatened by the spread of kauri dieback disease, which is killing off many of our trees. The thought of losing him is absolutely heartbreaking.

When we arrived at the forest, we ended up having a few words with a bunch of tourists who were nutting off about having to wash their feet and shoes with a special disinfectant set up at the entrance. The foot-washing is compulsory to stop the further spread of kauri dieback, and it is one of those things you have to do when you are in our forests. As far as I am concerned, when you are asked to do it, you don't argue about it.

We explained the reasoning behind it to the visitors, and in the end I said, 'Look, I know you're not from New Zealand, but this is what is happening, mate. If you won't wash your feet, then I am not going to let you in. I am a New Zealander, and this is my land, my forest. Please respect it.'

They did as they were asked, thankfully. After we got through that little scenario, we were approaching Tāne Mahuta when Pai stopped everyone, including some tourists, and did a karanga to show her respect to Tāne Mahuta. Talk about goosebumps – it was almost as if she was in trance. Everyone who witnessed it that day must have felt the emotion deep inside, even if they didn't understand what it was all about. It was another element of respect towards this almighty tree, along with the foot-washing to try to stop the spread of disease.

After that experience, Uncle happened to mention to Paitangi that he was looking for his kuia, and she suggested looking in a urupā (graveyard) where her friend is buried, which we would be driving past on the way home. She thought Uncle's whānau might be buried there.

So we called in at the church in the settlement of Ngawha and started wandering around. I stopped by one particular gravestone because I felt drawn to it, even though it was not the name we were looking for. Uncle came past and saw me standing there.

'That's not her, mate,' he said. 'Let's keep looking.'

I kept walking away, but each time I felt the urge to go back to that grave, even though it wasn't the right one. I was fighting with the situation, but in the end I left, and was on the other side of the burial ground when Uncle started waving at me across the gravestones. He was talking to two women who'd just turned up, and as I got closer I realised that he was standing next to the grave I had been drawn to.

He said to me 'I've found my kuia', and burst into tears.

It turned out it was the right grave after all, but the name was not familiar to Uncle because his grandmother had been buried under her maiden name. The two local women who had arrived at the cemetery asked Uncle if he needed any help, and when he told them he was looking for his kuia, and gave them her name, they just looked at him and said, 'She's our kuia, too.'

A couple of minutes later they were able to point out her grave to him: it was very close to where he was, but he hadn't realised because of the different name.

As if that wasn't emotional enough, Paitangi then did a karanga, followed by waiata (song) and karakia (prayer) to mark the occasion and pay our respects to Uncle's kuia. It was another extremely poignant moment. I never fail to be moved when I hear that cry.

Afterwards, as Uncle talked to his long-lost family members, I

I'm a proud New Zealander, and proud to celebrate our Māori culture.

It was a privilege to have Paitangi do my tā moko. They show my journey, my ancestors and where I come from.

The map I drew for Jo Stirling when her father-in-law was missing.

Boating to Cape Reinga. We had only planned a short trip, but nobody wanted to go home!

Left: Good friends and good fishing. An action shot of Uncle and Paitangi.

Below: Cape Reinga by sea. It's incredibly peaceful out here.

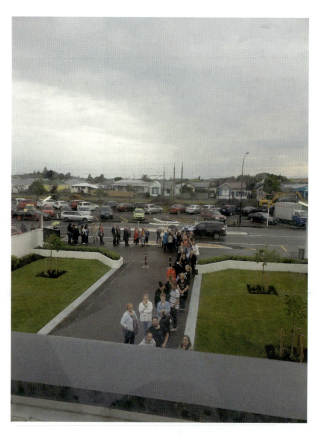

Left: Guests line up for one of my shows.

Below: Talking to a full house.

Above: Sight-seeing in Hollywood with two very special friends, Lisa and Karen.

Right: Piglet the cadaver dog outside the doctor's house in Los Angeles.

'Hanging loose' during a photo shoot.

sat down next to the grave, and next thing I knew I was pulling out weeds and polishing the headstone with my bare hands. After a while I looked up at Uncle and said, 'Matua, your kuia – she must have been a clean freak, right?'

There was something about the way I felt compelled to tidy up that made me think it was coming from his grandmother.

'Oh yes, she was,' he said.

Aren't spirit amazing?

Uncle says

I've been on some amazing adventures with Kelvin over the past couple of years, but the boat trip up to Cape Reinga was one of the best. I should have clicked where we were, but I didn't. It was such an incredible sight, seeing all the caves lining the cliffs, and the two oceans meeting. It's definitely a very spiritual place, but the weird thing is you don't feel spirit around you, because they have crossed over. Normally I have spirit around me all the time, but that day there was nothing. At first I thought, Have I done something wrong? Where have they gone?

Paitangi's karanga was one of the most special things I have ever witnessed, and I believe that her beautiful acknowledgement of those who have passed is why the boat was then surrounded by marlin. It was a sign of gratitude from spirit because we had paid our respects.

I had never seen a marlin up close until I saw the one Paitangi caught. What a magnificent creature. I couldn't bear the thought of keeping it, though – I kept saying, 'Let it go, let it go right now!' Fortunately, Kelvin put it back.

The day we went to Tāne Mahuta and then found my kuia was another day I will never forget. A group of us were staying at Kelvin's over the Christmas period and we decided to go on an excursion over to see Tāne Mahuta, which is absolutely awesome. When we stopped at the church on the way back, I wasn't sure if I would find my kuia because I had been to that graveyard before and hadn't managed to locate her.

A little bird flew onto the headstone next to me and I said to it, 'Okay, if I am meant to find my kuia, show me where she is.'

I watched to see where it would go, but all it did was hop to the next couple of gravestones. 'You're not much use,' I told it.

Then I got chatting to the two ladies who were there, and when I told them my kuia's name – Te Owai Pokaihau Rogers – they knew who I was talking about. She had been married twice and they were related to her through her other marriage. We had a little chat, then I walked off to continue looking at gravestones. I'd only gone a couple of metres when one of the women called out that they had found her. It had been confusing because she was buried under her maiden name. And the strange thing is, her grave was the last one the bird had gone to. It wasn't useless after all.

It was a relief to find my kuia, who was 109 when she died, because it meant her spirit would stop bothering me. She'd been with me for years, in my face wherever I went, because she wanted me to find her.

'Now you can leave me in peace!' I told her. She did, and actually a lot of things in my life fell into place afterwards. I did thank her for that.

I'm very grateful for these adventures I've had with Kelvin.

> I enjoy going on the road with him and attending his shows. I love seeing how he helps people. He has stayed very humble, and he recognises that this is not about him, it is about spirit and what they can do.
>
> When he is doing readings at his shows I will often connect with those spirit who have come through for him, and also pick up on what they are showing him. But I have no desire to get up on stage with him and do what he does. That's his place, not mine!
>
> Kelvin is very interested in learning new things, and over the years I have taught him a little about Māori culture and spirituality. He has embraced that, and when you do that, wairua then step in to help out. I take my hat off to him for his willingness to learn new stuff.
>
> That's what life is all about, a journey of learning. I feel that I am still learning things, even at my age, seventy-five. You are never too old!

My soulmate

Matua Tata – or Uncle – is not only my mentor when it comes to spiritual matters, he's my best mate, too. Our friendship goes back a long way, and we've been through a lot together. He helped me through a very difficult time when I was younger and got very sick coming off prescription drugs I had been given because the doctors thought the voices I was hearing meant I had ADHD. If it wasn't for him, I would not be here.

I'm not the only one to have been helped by Uncle over the years. He used to work in the mental health field years ago, and at the time I was able to observe some of the ways he helped the people under his care. He treated them like they were members of his own family, and the patients absolutely loved him. He made a massive difference to their lives and I am so proud of him.

He's had lots of different jobs in his life – working everywhere from Civil Aviation, the post office, the education sector, a medical clinic and a radio station through to being a 'garbologist' – rubbish collector! For many years he was also a caregiver for his late mum, Polly. He's picked up many skills along the way, one of which is his ability to relate to people and treat them respectfully. People could learn a lot from him.

Uncle is an incredibly wise person, and he's been able to give me so much valuable advice when it comes to spirituality. He's been through his own journey when it comes to accepting spirit, and has gained huge insights.

When he was a child, spirit used to regularly come to his room, and it frightened him. To his relief, his kuia, who was a tohunga, would chase them away. But it was still troubling, so his mother took him to a spiritual lady, who told him 'You are too young to be dealing with this', and effectively closed him down.

But when he got to 35, all of a sudden he started seeing and hearing spirit again. He couldn't understand what was going on – especially when a spiritual kapa haka group turned up in his bedroom – so he started saying his prayers. When he asked God 'Why me?', the answer he got was 'Why not?'

Uncle has come to terms with having spirit around, and he helped me to see that spirit are not scary or out to hurt us. Our family and friends who have passed over still love us and they want us to be happy, even if we are missing them so much that we can't imagine enjoying life ever again. His attitude is that life is a pleasure and we should do what we can to get the most out of it.

He's not only deeply spiritual, but he's bloody funny and I can truly be myself with him. You know how people go on about finding your soulmate, and they usually mean someone of whatever sex you're attracted to? Well, why can't your soulmate just be a person — regardless of gender or attraction or age — who you connect with on a deeper level? I'm pretty sure I have found my soulmate, and he's this Māori dude old enough to be my dad. I want to thank him for everything he has done. He gives such great advice, and he's also good at giving me a kick up the backside when I need it.

I'm proud to be his friend, and I'm looking forward to many, many more adventures with him.

An unspoiled spot

One thing that is really special about Māori culture is the connection the people have to the land. It plays a big part in their history and who they are, and they are very respectful of that. They are also very aware of how it gives them a home and provides them with sustenance, particularly in rural communities.

There are parts of the country where people live off their land, and they are understandably very protective of it. There's a place like that up north which is so beautiful that visiting it feels like a spiritual experience. It's so unspoiled that I am not going to tell you where it is, because I don't want to be responsible for lots of people turning up. It has managed to remain untouched for all this time; I think it should stay that way.

It's on the coast, and the locals not only live off the land but from the sea, too. They take what they need for a feed, no more. You can see snappers swimming through the mangroves with their backs out of water, and you can catch a 30-kilogram kingfish off the dock at high tide. When the tide's out, you can go and dig for monstrous great cockles in pure white shells. You can head out past a sand bar in your dinghy and go fishing. It really is a sacred spot.

Friends of mine who live there kindly let me and my crew stay with them a while back, and it was a beautiful experience. I have to admit that to start with we were getting some suspicious looks from some of the locals – they really are very careful about strangers, and I can't say I blame them. I certainly got a lot of attention when I took my boat out from there, caught a marlin and brought it back into the harbour. Apparently, it was the first time anyone has done that.

Normally I would have tagged the marlin and let it go. We had eight days of our holiday left and nowhere to store it, and I didn't feel like driving back to the Bay of Islands to get a chiller. But I said to my mates: 'What do you think, should we release it, or should we gift it to the locals and that way lots of people get a feed?'

It was a no-brainer. When we brought it back everyone came along to see what was going on, because it was such a rarity to see a marlin. The kaumātua tohunga (local priest) came along and blessed the kai (food) and thanked us. We kept a couple of slabs and gave the rest to the village. The people were rapt, and everyone stood around telling stories and having a good time. Ever since then, we have been really well received up there.

A couple of days beforehand we had seen a guy riding a horse who gave us a scary look when we said 'Kia ora, bro!' But the day after we caught the marlin, he came to where we were staying and said, 'Thanks so much for the kai, bro. I was just thinking, if I bring my other horses over, would the kids like to go for a ride down the beach?'

Of course, the answer to that was yes, and the kids in our group got to ride bareback over the sand on these horses. It was such a cool experience.

Again, it all boils down to respect. And to the understanding that in life there must be an exchange. If someone does something for you, you don't just take, you acknowledge, you give thanks and you give back (or pay it forward). Māori people get this, and so do Pacific Islanders — I saw these exchanges all the time when I lived in Tonga many years ago. It is a part of their culture. The rest of us could learn some important lessons from them.

Circle of life

I've had people say to me from time to time, 'KC, how can you be such a spiritual person and yet you go hunting and fishing all the time?'

Well, it's because this is how the food chain works. It is all part of the circle of life. I was raised to gather my own food, and everything I take, I take for kai. From boar and deer and even duck, through to marlin and snapper, I feed my family and sometimes the families of my friends with what I kill. It doesn't go to waste; it serves its purpose.

I never, ever take more than I need — most of the time I don't even take the limit imposed by law — and often I will throw back a lot of the fish I catch.

Before I go out fishing or hunting, I will say a karakia and ask to be kept safe while I'm out in the bush or on the ocean, and I will ask to be given the kai or kaimoana (seafood) I need. And sure enough, spirit always provides me with exactly what I need.

I know I have used this word a lot, but again it all comes down to respect. I have respect for these creatures that feed me, my family and my friends. It's not just about going out and having some fun, although I admit I enjoy the challenge and the bonding time spent with my mates fishing and hunting. I am always thankful for what I have been given, and I never take it for granted. This is what I mean by respect.

CHAPTER 13

Pain and payment

As you can tell, I am a really proud New Zealander. I am proud of our Māori culture, and I have always wanted tā moko, or traditional tattoos, to celebrate that and to depict my heritage.

I was extremely lucky to find an acclaimed tā moko artist, Paitangi, and privileged that she agreed to do my tā moko. Having it done the traditional way involves having faith in your artist. According to Māori beliefs, your story lies under your skin, and the ink of tā moko pulls it out. A good tā moko artist gets to know you a little beforehand, finds out about your journey and becomes attuned to your wairua and tūpuna, channelling them to produce an appropriate design. Once they start to work, your story begins to emerge on your skin, with everything having special significance.

This is what happened with me, and it was an awesome experience. The tā moko on my left arm depicts my hīkoi, or journey through this life. It shows where I come from: my maunga (mountain), which is Taupiri, and my awa (river), which is the Waikato. It depicts events that have been pretty major for me, such as Uncle coming into my life when I was really sick and basically saving me. My children and their stories also feature, and of course there is reference to spirit and the part it has played in my life.

On my right arm – which is my dominant arm – is the head of a taiaha or spear. Further up is the head of a waka (canoe), which is forever moving forward. The design also shows my ancestors, and the fact that they surround me. Really special to me are the 12 kete, or baskets of knowledge. I am blessed to have those – apparently getting those doesn't happen often to Pākehā fellas.

My tā moko shows that I am a human being and I am not invincible, but when it comes to spiritual matters I am protected, and there's an element of 'do not try to muck me around – ever'.

My tā moko go from my wrists to my shoulders, and I love them. But I have to admit, having them done hurt like hell. The left arm took two eight-hour days, and the right was 14 hours. You can't show your tā moko artist that you are in pain or they will stop tattooing. I managed to keep it together, and it was worth it.

And while the pain from the tā moko was bad, it was nothing compared with other pain I have experienced recently. For that, I can thank my boat.

A right pain in the back

Actually, I shouldn't blame my boat. It was a pure accident that I happened to fall off its roof and explode my back.

My game-fishing boat needed an overhaul, so my mates Adam

PAIN AND PAYMENT

and Grabby kindly offered to help out. We spent nine weeks on it, stripping it right back and then rebuilding it in my driveway. We spent many hours sanding it, rebuilding, repainting, putting in new cupboards and generally renovating it. All that was left to do was polish two aluminium rails at the very top, so I got up early one morning and climbed up with some rags and metal polish to get started.

One minute I was giving the rail a good rub; nek minute, I'd slipped backwards off the roof and was heading for the ground, headfirst. I put my leg out to stop myself, caught it on another rail and managed not to crash onto the concrete. But in the process I exploded some discs in my lower back.

We're talking serious pain here. The sort that rest doesn't fix. Over the next couple of weeks the pain just got worse. I had tests to see what damage I had done, including x-rays, but they didn't show anything. The painkillers I was on weren't working, and it got to the stage where I was in absolute agony. I could hardly dress myself in the morning; even sitting in my vehicle to take my daughter to the school bus was excruciating. After dropping her off I would cry all the way home because it hurt so much.

I then developed kidney pain and some other symptoms that I am not going to share with you – trust me, you don't want to know – at which point I was finally referred to a specialist. He sent me off for an MRI and told me I would need surgery to fix my back where the discs had exploded.

So off I went to hospital, desperate for the whole nightmare to be over. Getting onto the table for surgery, I slipped, and the pain was so excruciating I lost it. I was bawling like a baby, and wanted to curl up and die. A nurse had to come over and hold my hand while the anaesthetist was putting in the local anaesthetic before the epidural.

I remember her telling me: 'It's all right mate, just breathe through it, you are going to be okay.'

The anaesthetist had to give me two epidurals, and after a while he came back into the room and said, 'Uh, we've got a problem.' I was thinking 'Now what?' Your mind starts coming up with all these scary possibilities.

He said, 'Well, it's the theatre nursing staff. They all feel a bit nervous about you being here. We need to rectify this – would it be okay if I introduced you to them so they're a bit calmer?'

That was fine by me. I said hello to the nurses, and had a photo taken with them. There's me in my surgical gown and a hat like a shower cap, looking like death warmed up, and these smiling nurses standing around me.

When we eventually got into the operating theatre my surgeon was waiting for me. I told him I couldn't wait to have the op – I think I said something like, 'Let's go, bro: chop me up!'. I asked what people would have done back in the days before there was surgery to fix these kinds of problems. 'Probably either taken opium or drunk themselves to death,' he told me.

And things only got better: 'Thankfully we can do this surgery these days, because if we hadn't got you on the table now your nervous system would have started to shut down, followed by your organs. It could have all been over in a few weeks.'

Wow. That was scary news. I'd never been so pleased to be going under the surgeon's knife. I was told the operation should have taken around an hour and a half – in the end it took six and a half. They then wheeled me into the recovery room, where I spent another six or seven hours. Apparently while I was there I started reading for the nurses. I had no recollection of it afterwards; all I could remember was that somebody had brought me an ice block because my throat was sore.

But the next day, when I was up on a ward, a nurse came to see how I was doing, and said, 'Do you remember me?'

I had to admit: 'No, sorry, I don't.'

'I looked after you in recovery last night,' she said. 'I gave you an ice block.'

'Oh, I remember that!'

'You passed messages on to me.'

That I didn't recall. What had I said? 'I'm sorry, I hope I didn't offend you in any way.'

'No, you didn't,' she said. 'In fact, you changed my life. My partner, who has passed away, came and stood beside you while I was looking after you and you told me some things. I just wanted to say thank you.'

'You're welcome,' I told her.

I could vaguely remember talking to someone, but I had thought it was the drugs making me hallucinate. But no, it was spirit, unable to resist the opportunity to get me to pass on messages, even when I was coming around after major surgery.

It was a relief to have had the operation, but it wasn't the end of my problems, because afterwards, while I was recovering, I lost the use of my left leg. I couldn't lift it and had to drag it when I tried to walk. It was like a dead weight, and it was incredibly frustrating. In the end, I was able to get strength back in the leg by swimming in my pool. It took a while to get clearance to get in the water, because I couldn't risk my scars getting infected, but once I was allowed to get in the pool, exercising made a big difference.

The whole experience was an eye-opener. It makes you realise how quickly life can change in a split second, and how extreme pain can make life unbearable. It has also given me huge appreciation of the skill of our medical professionals, and made me thankful for the fact that I am mostly healthy again.

My back is not 100 percent, and I still have issues with it, so I have to be careful and not do anything stupid. I can't do things like jump from a chair down to the floor, as that would put too much pressure on my back. Damaging it like I did was frustrating, because I spent the best part of three months barely able to do more than lie on my couch, and I felt bad because I could hardly work. But it could have been far worse, and I am very grateful that I can still walk and be physically active.

It has also helped me understand what people go through when they suffer severe injuries and other health issues. My dad became a paraplegic a few years ago after he got septicaemia, or blood poisoning, first from getting pricked by a rose thorn and then after suffering bruising when he fell over his water-blaster. The toxins in his body went into his spinal cord, and as a result he is now paralysed. Saying it has been a very tough time for him is a major understatement. Having been through my issues, I can appreciate how hard it is when something happens that is beyond your control, and I am super proud of my dad for the way he has handled everything.

Working life

As I said, my back issues meant I had to take some time off work, which was frustrating as I hate letting people down. I know some people think I have a pretty cruisy life, turning up for shows a dozen or so times a month, where all I do is stand up in front of people and talk for a couple of hours. Piece of cake, right?

What they don't get is how exhausting it is for me to communicate with spirit and pass messages on to a room full of people. It requires a huge amount of concentration, which I try to explain to people by saying: 'Imagine for example how much effort you would need to drive from Auckland to Wellington in one go – in reverse.' Often it feels like I've done that after a show.

I have to concentrate hard to tune into spirit's frequency, so to speak, and then pay a lot of attention to what they are showing and telling me. It's not just an easy matter of saying 'Your gran says she's glad she was able to make you your wedding dress before she died'. Instead I might be shown a sewing machine, some white fabric, a church and a bridal bouquet, and I will have to figure it out from that.

Because of the way I work, I tend to get loads of spirit people turning up at the same time. The audience might see me standing on stage staring into space or mumbling to myself, but in fact I am trying to keep spirit under control. I might have an elderly couple for the lady I am reading for, plus a young man in spirit who died in an accident. There could also be a couple of babies in the background.

Then there's a woman who's turned up for a man in the middle of the front row and is trying to butt in, and a whole busload of people waiting to come through for a couple a few rows back. It can get chaotic, and I have to be on top of my game to sort it all out and make sure I am getting the right readings for the right people.

Afterwards I stay to sign copies of my books, and I don't leave the venue until every single person who wants a book signed has got my scribble in their copy.

When I do shows I usually schedule at least three or four in a row in a particular region of New Zealand to justify the travel expenses, and there can be a fair amount of driving between locations. So I do get home feeling pretty worn out.

When I'm not on the road, I'm not at home with my feet up – except for those occasions when my back packs up on me and I can't do anything other than lie on the couch. Being a single dad to my daughter Jade – my son Javan is now in his mid-twenties, can you believe it? – keeps me on my toes. When she's at school, there's plenty of business to tend to, from dealing with accountants to having discussions with publishers and TV people. My PA Crystal, who is also Jade's au pair, lives in my house, and she needs me to make decisions on topics like venues and dates for forthcoming shows. I also liaise a lot with Gemma, who runs my Facebook page and also does a lot of the organisational stuff. Without these two amazing people, my life would be chaos.

Then of course there are the things that come out of the blue. I get a lot of messages, usually via Facebook, from people asking for help on matters like finding missing people. In fact, as I've been working on this chapter I've had a message from someone whose mate was in a boating accident. He wrote: 'There's been no sign of his body – can you tell us where he is?'

As I've said, I help where I can. In the case of this particular guy, I knew his body would be found before I even had the chance to reply, and I was right. But there have been other occasions when I have dropped everything to try to assist, even driving long distances to meet with families. Obviously this can take a lot of time and it can also incur expenses, like petrol and accommodation.

I've never been paid for the work I've done finding missing people. I do it because I can, and because I want to help. It's not about money, and it wouldn't feel right to accept payment from families. Jo and Glenn Stirling said they wanted to give me something for what I did, not just finding Curly but for my support. 'You drove down to see us, there are fuel costs, accommodation,' they said.

I replied, 'No, it's all good.' But they got me a box of beer and I said, 'Okay, sweet, I'll accept that, thanks.'

John Mohi's family offered me a koha (donation), and when that happens you have to accept it because it would be disrespectful not to. So I took it, said thank you, and then I gave it back to them to help pay for his tangi (funeral).

This kind of work is funded with money I earn from doing my live shows, and that's one of the reasons I have done more shows in the past couple of years than in previous years. Contrary to popular belief, I am not raking it in – venue hire costs a small fortune and I have staff to pay as well as travel and accommodation expenses. I also have a mortgage and the usual household bills. But if I can use any leftover earnings to help pay for costs associated with helping people out, then I am happy to do that.

Of course, if I was offered paid work to be a consultant to police on missing persons and murder cases I would not turn that down. But I'm not holding my breath!

When kids see spirit

I get dozens of messages from people every day, and one of the most common (usually from mums) is asking for advice about kids who can see or hear spirit. They'll send me a message, or stick their hand up at one of my shows, and say, 'KC, my child is talking to people nobody else can see. It's freaking me out.'

When someone says that, I try to be as supportive as I can. I remind them that I am not unique in my ability to communicate with spirit. There are a lot of others who, to varying degrees, can see and hear wairua. That's one of the reasons why I hold workshops and retreats – to get people to explore these abilities and learn to use them.

People who can pick up on spirit and communicate with them are not crazy or nuts – although there are times when we feel like we must be, believe me! We are just more sensitive to spirit than others. Children in particular are more likely to be aware of wairua and able to connect with them, because children are much more open. They haven't been conditioned to think, Oh hey, how can talking to dead people be possible? However, it can be very scary for them – it's bad enough as an adult to try to get your head around the fact that dead people are talking to you and sending you messages, so imagine what it is like for a kid.

When mums ask me what to do, the first thing I usually say is to just accept them. Don't make a big deal out of it; talk to them about how this is something that they can do, but others can't, and there is nothing wrong with that. If they're old enough, reading my book *Finding the Path* may be able to help with advice on developing their abilities.

The crucial thing is to love them and support them and help them to find answers to their questions, either via someone like me and my books, or by talking to others at places like spiritualist churches. It is also important not to make a big deal out of what they can do. Don't turn them into a party trick and expect them to read for people as a form of entertainment. Be guided by how much they want to explore what they can do, and never exploit them.

There are some kids out there who are really struggling with what they are going through, and my heart goes out to them because I know how hard it is to feel different and weird. So I was really happy that a while back I was able to help a teenage boy who was having serious issues because he's very sensitive to spirit.

I heard about him from a friend, who said this kid was having such a bad time of it he was refusing to leave his room to go to school. I could instantly relate: school was a nightmare for me and not just because I'm dyslexic. Classrooms were packed with spirit hanging around with all the other pupils – and the teachers, too. It was overwhelming.

I got a phone number for this boy's mum, and one of the first things I said when I spoke to her was that he was going to be okay. 'We've got this, don't panic. I'm coming to your area in a few weeks – is it okay if I meet him?'

She was happy for me to do that, and as she was talking to me her dad came through in spirit. 'I hope you don't mind, but I need to tell you what your dad is saying,' I said, and off I went, flat-out, on a quick reading.

'How can you do that when we are just talking on the phone?' she said. 'That's amazing.'

I think that happened so that she could see what I am capable of. We arranged for me to see her boy in a few weeks, and they came to the hotel where I was staying.

He was only 13, and such a nice kid. He's a hard-working farm boy, respectful and kind, and yet he was scared to go to school because of all the spirit there. I told him what it was like for me as a kid, how I'd be walking around trying to figure out which people were real and which ones were spirit. Sometimes spirit would appear so clearly to me that it was hard to tell the difference.

It was also hard to concentrate in class because I could hear spirit all the time, and instead of focusing on the blackboard I'd be seeing the scenarios they were putting in my mind. It's difficult to pay attention to maths when your teacher's grandad is showing you the battles he fought in World War II.

I shared a few silly stories with this kid, and we laughed about this crazy gift we both have. I talked about how he can try to shut spirit down, and gave him affirmations to help with that.

After a couple of hours, when I figured he was ready to let loose, I said to him, 'Can you tell me who is with me in spirit?'

He hesitated. 'I don't know if I should do that.'

'Look, mate, there's no need to be scared. You're safe here,' I reassured him.

He took a deep breath. 'Well, there's this bloke with white hair, and he's standing beside you. He's got a Swanndri on, a red-and-black chequered one. He's also wearing a strange hat and corduroys – he loves those cords. He used to go hunting with you, and his name starts with M. M-O . . . I can't get the rest.'

He had my granddad, Monty, down to a T. And then this 13-year-old boy went on to tell me other details, and 90 percent of it was information that nobody else knows. I've met mediums from all over the world and none of them has ever been able to get my koro to that level. But this boy was nailing it, and he blew me away.

He talked for a few minutes, then he said, 'Oh, I'm being told I've got to be quiet now.'

That was all good. He had done what he needed to do, and I hoped the experience had helped him to come to terms with the ability that he has. As he and his mum were leaving, she said to me, 'KC, I'd like to pay you for your time.'

I said, 'Don't be silly, I am only too happy that I could help out.'

'But we need to do something — you've given up so much time,' she insisted.

I was just as adamant. 'No, this has been my pleasure.'

Then she said, 'You like hunting, right? I've got a huge farm that nobody goes hunting on. You'd be most welcome to come down with your mates and go for a hunt.'

Wow, what an offer! I said to her, 'I would love to take you up on that — on one condition. Can your son come hunting with me?'

His face lit up. 'I love hunting, but I'm not very good at it,' he said.

'I'll teach you,' I promised him.

I was so chuffed with that — I honestly did not expect anything from them, and to get to go hunting and to teach this kid, who reminds me so much of my younger self, about a pastime I love, is a huge bonus.

I'm about to go down there soon, and as if hunting on a farm that nobody has shot on before is not enough, I have also been given one of the most special gifts I have ever received. A package from this boy arrived in the mail, and I opened it to find that he had saved up his pocket money to buy me a custom-made hunting knife, and he had my name carved into the deer-antler handle. The note with it said: *KC, I can't thank you enough for helping me, so I had this made for you. I hope you don't mind.*

PAIN AND PAYMENT

When I saw that, I cried. What an awesome, thoughtful thing to do. It's absolutely beautiful, and I am saving it to use that first time we go hunting together.

The other thing I have got out of this experience that makes me very emotional is knowing that he is coping so much better with life now. He can go to school and the supermarket and the movies with his mates because spirit no longer freaks him out. He's doing his affirmations, his spiritual mahi (work) and he's figuring things out.

That makes me very happy. It's the best payment.

CHAPTER 14

A warning from spirit

Life was pretty good for a couple getting a reading from me at one of my Auckland shows. They had just got married and built themselves a beautiful new home in the countryside. Now they were in the big smoke catching my show before heading off the next day on an extended overseas trip. Lucky people.

But while I was reading for them, spirit was showing me water pipes, and an on/off switch.

'Have you turned the water off at the mains in your place?' I asked.

'No. Why?' was the reply I got back.

'Because most people, when they go away for long periods of time, turn the water off. It's called taking precautions.'

They didn't seem worried. 'It's a new house, it will be all right.'

'No, it won't be,' I told them. 'There's a problem with your plumbing and it isn't going to be pretty.'

'Well, there's not a lot we can do about it now,' they said. 'We're not going home, we're off to the airport tomorrow.'

'Is there somebody you can call to turn the water off for you?'

I was being persistent, but that was because spirit was telling me it was important.

'Nah, don't worry. It'll be sweet,' they said.

It wasn't sweet. They arrived home from their fantastic holiday to find a pipe had burst in the roof, spraying water everywhere and filling the loft up like a swimming pool. Once the water reached a certain level, the ceiling could no longer bear the weight and had given way. The place was a mess.

I don't usually make a habit of issuing warnings during readings. As I have said many, many times, I don't predict the future. I am not a fortune-teller, I can't give you the Lotto numbers and I cannot tell you if you are going to end up married to that cute guy from the IT department.

However, sometimes spirit does choose to show me things that haven't happened yet, and if it is a situation where there is a problem — like bursting water pipes — then it should be taken as a warning. I don't mean to stress anyone out, but spirit has shown me these images for a reason, and I need to pass the message on. Usually that message is that you need to take steps to avoid these things happening — or at least mitigate their severity. If you get a warning, do something about it.

Many years ago a friend came to visit me when I was living at a West Coast beach near Auckland. As I walked her to her car when it was time for her to leave, I had an image of the driver's side of the car stoved in, as if she'd been in an accident. 'It might be a good idea not to speed on your way home,' I told her.

She said she didn't drive fast.

'Yeah, but please be careful, because there's going to be a problem – I can see the whole side of your car stoved in.'

She promised she would take it easy, and set off. It was a windy road back to town, and it was raining. Unfortunately, somebody had spilt oil or diesel on the road, and as she came around a corner she hit this patch of slippery stuff and spun out. She ended up in a ditch across the road.

Just as I had seen, the driver's side of the car was all smashed up; it was a write-off. But my friend was okay, other than being a little shocked. Luckily, she had been following my advice and not driving fast. If she had been speeding, she could have been badly injured. So while the accident had still happened, because she had listened to my warning and taken it seriously, the outcome ended up a lot better than it could have been.

Most of my friends know to trust me when I warn them about something. And those who don't soon learn.

I said to a mate once, 'Bro, you know that fella at work who looks like . . .' I gave a description. 'Well, you need to watch yourself, he's stealing stuff.'

My mate said, 'Nah, he wouldn't do that. Not him.'

'Just be careful with your things,' I told him.

A month later he said to me, 'Bro, that fella you told me about? He got sacked for stealing. Turns out, the boss had put cameras up and they caught him.'

I don't like to say I told you so, but . . .

When I give people warnings at my shows, I usually get one of two responses. There are those who go into panic mode. I will say, 'Look, just because I have seen your kid coming off a bike doesn't mean that they should never ever get on a bike again. Just make sure they wear a helmet, and if they're going down a steep hill, maybe they should get off and push the bike down rather than risk coming off at breakneck speed and doing serious damage to themselves.'

Then there are those, like the people with the burst water pipe, who are like 'Yeah, whatever'. If they don't want to believe me, that's their choice. If it is something fairly minor, I restrict it to something like: 'You might want to start parking your car in the driveway instead of on the road, because it is going to get hit.' After all, a car can easily be replaced.

But if it involves someone's health or safety, and I am getting a really strong message from spirit, then I can get pretty insistent on spirit's behalf. I will eyeball the person and say: 'Look, I know you don't understand this and you probably think I am talking a load of nonsense, but please, tell your husband to be extra careful any time he is going up a ladder.'

I told a woman at a show that she was going to have two kids one day – as it happened, she was pregnant at the time – and once she became a mum, there was one really important thing she had to do.

'Living in New Zealand, with so many beaches and lakes and rivers and basically water everywhere, it is really important that we all know how to swim. When your children come into this world, please make the effort to get them to swimming lessons from a very early age.'

Her grandad was with me in spirit, and he kept telling me it was crucial. 'He is saying if we don't do this, something very serious could happen. Swimming lessons are paramount, and sooner rather than later.'

She explained that she can't swim very well herself, even though she grew up with a pool.

'If you're bad at it, the likelihood of you teaching them to swim is pretty low,' I pointed out. 'That's why he's saying, "Get them lessons, please."'

Grandad hadn't finished there with the warnings. He also mentioned a car crash involving friends of her partner, and it was due to drink driving. 'I'm pretty sure they survive, but it is going to be a big wake-up call. When you get home, give your partner a bit of a serve to make sure that his mates don't get on the turps after work. He has got to be in charge of that, and there is one person who needs to hear this more than the others.'

The final warning was about the exposed electrical wires all over their home, which they were in the process of renovating. 'Tidy them up and put some tape around them. I keep getting shown wires and electrical stuff for some reason, so you need to be vigilant.'

It was a lot for this woman to take on board, and I did feel like I was being a bit of a negative Nigel, but it was what her grandad wanted me to say. Fortunately she took the warnings really well; she didn't freak out, nor did she dismiss me. I hope as a result she was able to avoid these scenarios, or reduce the severity of them.

If you ever come to one of my shows and get a message like this, please remember that I'm not just saying these things because I like the sound of my voice, I'm saying them because spirit wants me to, and there's usually a very good reason for that.

So how do I know?

I can hear you thinking, So if KC reckons he can't predict the future, how can he warn someone about something that hasn't happened yet? Good question.

I see these things because spirit can see the future, and sometimes they will show me on a need-to-know basis. In my book *Taking the Journey* I explained how we all write our story, with our Creator, before we get here. We each have a book containing our story, and each of our books is sitting up in heaven on an ornate stand. Your loved ones in spirit can look at the book and see what is going to happen. If they get permission from the Creator, they can come through and give us a warning. And they don't only do that through a medium like me, usually they will try to warn you directly. The trouble is you may not realise it is a warning from spirit, and you may not listen.

Have you ever had a close call? An incident where if you had changed lanes on the motorway just five seconds later the outcome would have been very different? Often people will say after having a close shave on the road: 'Jeez, I don't know what it was, but something made me turn the steering wheel.' Or they might say: 'I didn't go to that party because something didn't feel right, and just as well – a huge fight broke out.'

Those intuitive feelings or thoughts that pop into your mind are not random. They're spirit. Trust me on this.

Some people might even hear a voice or have a sense of a loved one being with them when something like this happens. A friend of mine swears she heard her grandfather saying 'Stop!' seconds before she was about to reverse her car into a post she couldn't see. I can tell you 100 percent, that was her pop looking out for her.

Although hearing a voice doesn't happen for all of us, spirit are still communicating with us via our gut feelings. You know what I mean, that kind of gnawing feeling in your stomach that makes you think, Okay, I'm not sure about this. If this happens to you, go with it. And don't forget to say: 'Kia ora, [Nan, or whoever it is], I guess you are trying to tell me it's not a good day to go out on the motorbike. Thanks for that.'

If you want to be more attuned to your wairua so you can get these warnings if and when you are meant to, try spending five minutes a day meditating and talking to your loved ones in spirit. Remember, they love you, and if you let them they will do their bit to keep you as safe as they are able to.

When I don't get warnings

Warnings are like other pieces of information from spirit: I don't get them if I am not meant to. Just like sometimes I get absolutely nothing about a missing person, or a murder case, or I can't tell you where Nana's long-lost engagement ring is, there are plenty of occasions when spirit doesn't issue a warning for me to pass on to someone, even when you think they would really need it.

Or sometimes I might see a situation potentially happening, but I don't get crucial details that might have made a huge difference if only I'd been able to pass them on.

I've written before about Freda, an older lady I read for over 10 years ago now, who had suffered a lot of tragedy in her life and lost lots of loved ones. Her son had committed suicide, and I was able to pass on a message from him, which made her very happy. While I was talking to her, I was seeing images of a house fire, which worried me.

'Look, this is important – has there ever been a house fire in your family's history?' I asked.

Freda sat there for a moment, then said no.

'You've never been in a fire?'

'No, never.'

I was feeling quite agitated without really knowing why, and I couldn't force the issue.

A few months later I found out that she'd gone home after my show, all excited about the contact with her son, had a long chat with her neighbour, and then gone to bed. During the night an electrical fire broke out in the house, and she died. I felt so sad when I heard that. I had known there was a fire, but not that it would happen that very night and that it would be fatal. Looking back, I think that if I had been meant to do something that would have prevented Freda from dying, spirit would have allowed me to do that. But it didn't happen like that.

It's been hard for me because there have been times when I've felt guilty over things that have happened to people. In the past I have thought, Why couldn't I have done something to stop that? When friends of mine have died, I have thought, Why wasn't I able to warn them?

But I have come to understand that I just wasn't meant to. If I don't get a warning before something awful happens, it's because they have their path to follow, and it is not my place to interfere with that journey.

My friend Helen, who owned a zoo in South Auckland, died in 2012 when she was crushed by an elephant, Mila. It was a huge shock, and I was absolutely devastated – Helen was a lovely lady who really cared for the animals in her zoo. Many had been rescued from a lifetime of abuse, and they were very well looked after, as Helen was not only a huge animal lover but also very experienced in animal care.

The weird thing was that for about a week beforehand, I kept seeing images of elephants everywhere and couldn't figure out why. I did not connect them at all with Helen, and, as hard as it was, I had to accept that her journey was mapped out for her and I couldn't have changed that.

I wish other people would also accept that sometimes I just can't do anything about events that are about to happen. Once I was in a shop with my son Javan when a staff member approached me and suddenly started asking a lot of questions. I can't remember now exactly what she wanted to know, just that she had an issue with someone in her family. She really got in my face, and it was totally inappropriate, so I said, 'Look, I'm sorry but I can't help you.' And I couldn't, I wasn't getting anything – most probably because of her behaviour.

A few weeks later I was back in the same shop when the woman came up to me again. This time she was downright angry and aggressive; I'd even go so far as to say abusive. It turned out that the person she had spoken to me about on the previous occasion had just died, and she was having a go at me because I hadn't told her that was going to happen. Somehow it was all my fault.

'If you had told me they were going to die, I could have made my peace with them,' she said. She was clearly furious with herself for not having reconciled, and she was taking out her fury on me. While I'm sorry she had been through that, flipping her lid at me wasn't going to help. It's a very hard way to learn a lesson, but maybe now she knows that it is not a good idea to hold grudges. If you have an issue with someone, sort it out, because you never know what could be around the corner.

One hell of a warning

I was outside one day mucking around in my garden when I started feeling unwell. I went inside and was so dizzy and lightheaded that I had to lie down on the couch. I thought, Oh no, what is going on? I felt as if spirit was trying to show me something, so I closed my eyes and saw this whole sequence of events happening through my third eye.

Remember Lisa, the director of the TV show I have been working on in the United States? In my vision she was at home alone, as her wife Karen was away at a conference. I could see that she had gone into the bathroom to have a shower, and that the ranch slider at the back of the house had been left partially open.

I could see a pair of size seven shoes, along with trackpants and a T-shirt, which are not normally what Lisa wears. And I also saw a man with a knife getting into the house via the ranch slider.

In my vision, Lisa came out of the bathroom because she heard a noise, and went to the back door. The man attacked her, and slit her throat.

It was awful, but I knew I was seeing this for a reason: I had to let her know that her life could be in danger.

It's not an easy conversation to have. You don't just ring someone and say, 'Hey, mate, I think someone might try to murder you.'

I had to establish that I'd got things right, so first I asked Lisa if Karen was going to be away, and she said yes, Karen was going to a conference that weekend. I also asked Lisa if she happened to change into trackpants and a T-shirt when she was relaxing at home, and again she said yes, she did.

In the end I just came out with it, and told her she either needed to leave the house while Karen was away or barricade it up, because I had seen her being attacked with a knife in my vision.

It was weird issuing instructions to my director, but I knew it was very important that I did it. Spirit weren't mucking around.

Lisa says

The call from Kelvin came out of the blue. He said, 'Don't freak out, but is there anyone who is angry with you, or means you harm?'

I said no, not that I could think of. Then he asked who wore a size seven shoes: me or Karen?

'That's me,' I said.

It kind of ended there, but about two hours later he called again.

'So here's the deal. Spirit wouldn't be telling me this unless you're meant to be saved, so don't freak out. But I have had a vision of you dead – throat cut. I don't know what this is about, but here's what you have to do. When you are at home, make sure everything is locked up. All the doors, all the windows. Set the alarms, do everything you need to do to stay safe.'

I said 'Okay', and I did as I was told.

Karen went out of town, and although I had done everything Kelvin had asked, I still felt a little freaked out. Thankfully nothing happened, which was a relief.

When Karen got back a couple of days later, she went to our local market, and while she was standing in line waiting to be served, she heard the cashier talking to another customer about a murder in the shopping centre across the street. We don't have cable, so we don't watch the news, and we didn't know what had happened.

It turned out that a woman had been stabbed in her SUV in the parking garage of the mall. It's not even a mile from our house, and we go there all the time. A week before Kelvin called, I had been in that parking lot as the sun was going down and I'd got a creepy feeling. I remember getting into my car and thinking, No more coming here anymore when it's this late.

The area we live in is usually very safe – her murder was the first here in nine years. So it was really horrible. But what really got us was that this woman looked like me. Her hair was similar to mine. She was wearing a T-shirt and warm-up pants. And her shoes were size seven.

For all we know, the killer could have been around here. The fact that I'd locked up everything like Kelvin had instructed me to may have saved my life. I still wonder if that could have been me.

LISTEN TO SPIRIT

> I still follow the guidelines KC laid out that day about the possible threat to my situation and my safety. The doors and windows are locked at all times when I'm home alone working, because the killer has never been caught and one never knows when he may try again. It's not that I live in fear, but I believe in KC enough to listen to what he tells me I need to do in order to stay safe.

A case of mistaken identity?

A CCTV photo taken of the murder victim shows her heading to her car shortly before she was killed, and the resemblance to Lisa is uncanny. She is wearing the same clothes I saw in my vision, and the same shoes.

That poor lady was found with multiple stab wounds, and her throat was slashed. So far, no one has been charged with her murder, and the police are saying it appears to have been a random attack. From what I understand, she was a much-respected and loved mother and grandmother, with no enemies, no criminal background, nothing that would make her the target of a vicious killer.

I don't know why that woman was killed. I don't know who did it. But I can't help wondering, because of the vision I had, whether it was a case of mistaken identity. Did someone try to get into Lisa's house, and when they couldn't did they kill this woman thinking it was her? That's just a theory; I have no proof. It's terrible to even think about that being the case, that Lisa may have been the intended victim. But I think there is a connection to the vision I had, and that spirit showed me what they did for a reason. That reason was to warn Lisa, and possibly save her life.

CHAPTER 15

Random readings

I was in my shed one day trying to tidy it up – a never-ending job, you should see the state of it – when Gemma sent me a text.

'Hey KC, look at my new tattoo,' she wrote, alongside a photo of a half-done tattoo. Then she sent through another picture, this time of her tattooist, bending over her foot and working on the tattoo.

It wasn't a very clear image of him, you could only see half of his face, and his eyes weren't visible. But it wasn't him my attention was drawn to when I looked at the photo; it was a guy I could see standing next to him, who I could tell had recently committed suicide.

At this point I need to mention that this is something I don't usually do. I don't normally pick up on dead people from photos, especially photos they are not actually in. But for some reason, this guy in spirit came through to me and told me how he had died, and I figured I was meant to talk to Gemma's tattooist about him.

So I messaged her back and said, 'Do you think your tattooist would be open to me telling him about his mate who committed suicide and is in the photo with him?'

She said she'd ask. It's a pretty random thing to come out with, but Gemma said to the tattoo guy: 'Do you know who Kelvin Cruickshank is?'

He said yes, the fella from *Sensing Murder*.

'Is it okay if I tell you something he has just said to me after seeing the photo of you?' she asked.

He said he was a bit sceptical about that kind of stuff, but why not? What did I want to say?

Well, off I went on one of the most unusual readings I have ever done. It was all carried out via text, with me looking at the photo, and then sending what I was getting from spirit to Gemma, who relayed it to the guy doing her tattoo. The tattooist's mate gave me all kinds of information, including telling me that his friend was so grief-stricken that he'd bought a fishing rod, because he'd heard fishing was a good stress-buster. But he had no idea how to work it, so had ended up just sitting with it on the wharf, catching nothing.

Apparently, that was spot-on. The tattooist admitted to Gemma: 'I heard that fishing helps with stress, so I tried. How did he know that?'

I knew because his mate was there with him on the wharf that day, and told me about it.

Among the details his mate in spirit gave me was a really important message for another friend who had been so gutted by his death that he was struggling with suicidal thoughts himself.

I texted Gemma: 'Please tell the tattooist to tell his other mate that their friend who died is okay and not to worry so much. The mate who is still here needs to lift his head up and get on with life.'

The tattooist confirmed that their other friend was really doing it hard. Later he told Gemma that he'd gone over to see that mate after the reading from me and passed on the message.

'You might have saved his life with that message, KC,' Gemma told me.

I don't know about that, but I do know that there was a reason why this dead guy came through to me via the photo, and why he mentioned the third mate. I think the tattooist and the other guy really needed to hear from their dead mate, to help with their grief.

Gemma said to me later, 'That was epic! In all the years I have known you, I have never seen you do a reading from a photo before. You never do this. And everything you said was absolutely spot-on!'

It wasn't me, though, it was spirit, and when they need to pass on a message they do whatever they can to be heard and seen. They're the ones who are amazing.

I could do without them interrupting me when I am trying to clean my shed, though. It's still a mess.

Roadside reading

Like the situation with Gemma's tattooist, every now and then I find myself doing random readings for complete strangers. Often they happen when I am least expecting them.

One of them took place while I was away doing shows, and Crystal, who had just come to work as my PA and Jade's au pair, was making her first trip with me. We were driving from Gisborne to Napier when we came up behind a long line of backed-up traffic. Obviously something pretty major had happened up ahead – nothing was moving. Someone from a car further up came walking down the road, and told us that a truck had overturned and was blocking the road. I was not thrilled to hear that it could be up to two hours until a crane could be brought in to move the truck.

We were in the middle of nowhere, and there was nothing to do but hang out and wait. As we sat in the car I could hear the words 'Roadside reading, roadside reading' in my head. I thought, Okay, whatever.

'Since we are going to be here for ages we might as well get out of the car and stretch our legs,' I said to Crystal.

We were leaning on the back of the car when the couple in the vehicle behind got out to let their dog go for a pee, and I started talking with them. They didn't say anything about recognising me, and it was nice to have a normal conversation with people who weren't uptight about what I do for a living, or anxious for me to put them in touch with their dead relatives.

But it wasn't long before I could tell that I was going to have to say something about what I did – because I had a rather insistent spirit on my hands.

'Do you guys know what I do, by any chance?' I asked when the opportunity arose.

'Yeah, we've seen you on TV,' said the woman. 'But we thought it would be nice not to say anything.'

'Thanks, that's really respectful of you,' I said. 'But the thing is, I've got a bit of a problem.'

'What's that?' she asked.

'I've got someone here who really wants to talk to your partner. Is that okay?'

The guy shrugged and said, 'Sweet.'

'Your mum's here,' I told him, and he froze.

'She wants me to tell you some things. Do you mind?'

He took a deep breath, and said okay, and off I went. It was really quite an intense reading, and the information was coming through thick and fast from the mother. She told me that her son had been living overseas, and when he got the call to say she wasn't doing well he'd headed straight back to New Zealand to try to see her before she died. He got there half an hour after she passed, and was gutted.

She was a real character, his mum, and she started telling jokes to try to cheer her boy up. She told me he was doing it tough. He didn't have a job and he was depressed. But the worst thing was that his ex-partner had driven a big wedge between him and their kids, and was trying to turn them against him. That was cutting him to bits.

'It's a bad situation at the moment, mate, but it is going to get better, I promise you,' I told him. 'Your kids love you and they miss you. The toxicity is going to start to clear. You're going to get a job, and you are going to be able to save the money to fly your kids out here, don't worry about that. Please hang in there, mate – trust that your mum is going to sort this out for you.'

The guy was leaning on the bonnet of his car as I spoke to him. He lifted his sunnies, and I could see that he was crying.

'I can't believe this,' he said. 'It's all true. My ex-partner has alienated my kids and it is breaking my heart. But to hear my mum say there is light at the end of the tunnel . . . This is off the charts! You have no idea what you have done.'

He stood there and cried, and I hugged him and cried, too. It was incredibly emotional, and it all unfolded by the side of the road in the middle of nowhere.

Spirit had warned me with the words 'roadside reading', but I had no idea it would be so intense, or would mean so much to that guy.

When Crystal and I got back in the car, she said to me, 'That was just so cool, KC. Wow! He transformed right in front of us. When he first got out of the car you could see how low his energy was, he seemed really down. But by the time you finished talking to him, that big black cloud hanging over him had gone away. It was like he was a different person.'

I've noticed lately that people who need help from spirit like that guy do seem to magically turn up in my life. And they seem to be good people who are worthy of help.

Things had really got on top of that guy, and he was broken. His lovely mum desperately wanted to help fix him, and no way was she going to miss out on the chance to do that via me. I hope things have improved with his kids and on the job front, and that the horrible cloud of depression has lifted for good.

His mum may be gone from this world, but she still loves him, and she will do whatever it takes to help her boy. I'm stoked if I was able to play a part in that.

When spirit play Cupid

I don't make a habit out of doing readings for my friends, but every now and then, if the situation is right, I find myself compelled to say something to one of them.

I met Kath and her husband, Si, at Thirsty Thursday, an informal gathering that my mates Adam and Jodie hold at their place every week. It involves a few drinks – you can turn up for a quiet glass of wine and a quick catch-up, or sometimes you can go pretty hard out and end up staying the night so you don't drink and drive.

From the moment I saw Kath I could see that she had the spirit of a man with her, and he told me he was her first husband. He hassled me quite a lot about passing on a message to her, but I never said anything because it wasn't an appropriate setting to do that. Then one night she said to me, 'Would you mind doing me a favour? Can you read for me?'

'So you'd like me to tell you about your husband who was

tragically taken from you?' I replied.

Her mouth dropped open. I had hit the nail on the head.

'We won't do it here, but why don't you come over to my place?' I said. At last, here was my chance to get this guy off my back. He was eager to talk to her, and when we sat down to do the reading he came through loud and clear. He had been tragically killed in an accident, and it had broken her heart – they had fallen in love when they were young and had been devoted to each other.

I did the reading with Kath and was able to pass on lots of messages from this guy. I think it gave Kath a lot of comfort, and the next time I saw Si, he said, 'Thank you so much for what you said to my wife, she's so happy.'

One of the interesting things that came out of the reading was that Kath's first husband told me to tell her: 'Hey, it's okay that you are with Simon, because I put him in front of you.'

Si told me they had met when he was so busy looking into his wallet while he was standing in a queue that he had banged into Kath.

'You were meant to,' I told him. 'Her husband reckons he made it happen.'

This is an example of how spirit do what they can to help us to be happy. They don't want us to grieve forever, they want us to get on with life and make the most of it.

I've lost count of the number of times I have done a reading for someone who has lost a partner or spouse, and their loved one has come through to say 'I arranged for you to find the new person in your life'.

It's interesting how many people say: 'I always had the feeling that that was the case, but I wasn't sure. Now I know – thanks, KC.'

Don't thank me, thank spirit.

Needled into passing on messages

I'm pretty good at separating my work from my home life, and if spirit turn up while I am on my downtime I'll usually close them down and say: 'No, sorry, now's not the time.' But sometimes they are pretty insistent, in which case the only way I can get rid of them is to pass on what they want to say to their loved one.

This happened a while back with a guy called Smithy, who is friends with my good mate Shane. I met Smithy for the first time when a group of us went over to his house to have a drink or three. This older lady, who I could tell was Smithy's mum, was there with us in spirit all night. In fact, while we were outside talking and having a few drinks, she was sat inside on the couch, knitting frantically.

She kept saying to me, 'Will you talk to my boy, please?' I said to her (in my head), 'No, I can't: I'm off-duty and I'm having a wine.'

Normally I don't do readings if I've had alcohol, as it can affect my ability to concentrate on what I am getting from spirit. So I tried to ignore her. But the more I ignored her, the angrier she got, and the faster she was knitting. Those knitting needles were going crazy!

It wasn't until a lot of people had left and there were just a few of us remaining – all of them people I trust – that the opportunity to do what she wanted arose. Smithy said something along the lines of 'I wish my mum was here, she'd love this wine'.

I said, 'Um, funny you should say that, because she is actually here.'

Next thing, I was sitting next to Smithy, telling him what his mum wanted me to pass on. It was quite emotional, because there were some things he had been carrying around with him that he needed to let go of, and you could see the weight lifting from him as I told him what his mum was saying. Several other family members popped along, too, and I was able to give him their names.

My mate Shane had never seen me do a reading, and he was

looking at me as if to say 'Holy crap! How are you doing this?'

I don't make a habit of it, but sometimes you've just got to do what spirit wants you to do. It makes for an easier life.

Spirit-free zones

I often get asked if I can pick up on spirit anywhere at any time. The answer to that is yes, with a couple of notable exceptions. As you've already seen, I didn't pick up on spirit when I went up to Cape Reinga by boat. That was because they had all crossed over and were making their way to the next world.

The other place where I can go if I need a bit of peace and quiet from dead people – and you may find this hard to believe – is a cemetery. True. I don't get spirit talking to me in a urupa because it is holy ground. I realised this when I was a kid and struggling with having spirit around me all the time. I used to go to a cemetery, sit beside a grave where it was nice and peaceful, and cry my eyes out. At least I knew I wouldn't be bombarded with voices there.

Later on, when I was living in Rotorua and my life was a mess because these dead people wouldn't leave me alone and everyone (me included) thought I was nuts, the cemetery was the one place I could go to get away from the craziness.

While I don't have lots of spirit around me when I am in a graveyard, sometimes I may get some ideas or images popping into my head – like when I was drawn to the gravestone that turned out to be Uncle's kuia. And I did once have a conversation with my nanny when I went to visit her grave when I was a kid. I sat there saying 'I miss you, my nan', and I heard her say 'You know this is not where I am'.

'So why can I hear you?' I asked her.

'Because I've come to tell you that this is not where I am – but you know that, boy!'

So she came to tell me she wasn't there. Right . . . .

I know some people are freaked out by cemeteries and the thought that people's remains are buried there. But believe me, because they are sacred places, they are very peaceful and safe. And cemeteries are also where I can find absolute solace, which I appreciate.

At the other end of the scale, there are places I avoid as much as possible because they are teeming with spirit. These include battlefields and the sites of mass deaths. For example, I really had a hard time of it when I went to the Coliseum in Rome because of the lost souls hanging around there.

I could never go somewhere like Auschwitz, where you can do a tour of the former concentration camp. It's hugely emotional and upsetting for most people; it would have me in bits.

And on a day-to-day basis, one place I find it really hard to be is a hospital. I hate them, and not only because I've had some pretty horrendous experiences in them and they're associated with pain. Even if I am just going to visit someone, the minute I walk through the doors I start spinning out because spirit is everywhere. The corridors are full of them, so are the stairwells, the lifts and the rooms. Either they are people who have just passed away, or they are spirit waiting for a loved one who is about to cross over. I can't escape them.

If I have to go to hospital to see someone I will put on my headphones, crank up my music, and walk in with my head down so I don't make contact with any of them. If they realise I can see them, then it is all on – they're in my face.

Remember the movie *The Sixth Sense*, where the kid could see dead people walking around with terrible wounds? Well, welcome to my world. It really can be overwhelming.

A while back my mum was in hospital, and when I went to visit her, from the moment I got in the door, I was like a helicopter, just spinning out. There was spirit everywhere. Because the elevator wasn't working, I had to go up the stairs and they were full of spirit walking up and down. I got into the corridor leading to my mum's room, and there were so many people I was thinking, 'Which ones are real and which ones aren't?'

A guy mopping the floor looked up at me and went 'Kia ora, bro!' I said 'Kia ora,' back, and then I gave him a quick prod to check he was real.

He went, 'You're that fella on TV. Ow!'

I said, 'Yeah, that's me. Sorry about that.' But at least I knew he wasn't a ghost.

I literally had to push past spirit people as I went down the corridor to my mum's room.

She was doing okay, but sadly the elderly lady in the bed next to her was not in a good way, in fact she was dying. And the room was full of her wairua, standing around waiting for her to pass over.

I handed my mum the flowers I'd got her, asked how she was, had a quick chat and then got out of there as fast as I could. I think I was there for all of eight minutes, but I just couldn't handle all those dead people.

The worst time was when I went to visit my mum when she was working as the chaplain at a hospital. I met her in her office, and she said, 'Let's go to the cafeteria for a cup of tea.'

I followed her along the corridors and after a little while I noticed a lot of spirit people wandering around with horrible injuries and body parts missing.

'You've brought me past the morgue!' I said to her. 'Thanks very much!'

I think I must have power-walked to the elevator, trying to get away from them. I know talking to dead people is what I do, but when there are so many of them, and they're all going 'Help me, help me' because they want me to pass on messages to their loved ones, then I am going to give Usain Bolt a run for his money. Time and place, folks, time and place.

Over the years I've learned several ways of keeping spirit from hassling me so much. The main one is doing a karakia to shut them down. While it works a lot of the time, there are occasions when they still get through.

And, as I've said, I also tend to wear headphones and listen to music a lot, because that helps to keep them quiet, or more accurately it stops me from hearing them. I'll often do this in public places like airports because it makes life a little easier.

Another thing I do is call out to spirit whenever I drive past one of those roadside crosses at the site of a fatal accident. If I don't pay my respects by saying 'Kia ora, bro', there's a chance they'll end up in the car with me, telling me all about what happened to them. But if I acknowledge them respectfully, they will leave me alone.

There are definitely times when spirit come to me – perhaps when I am tired or trying to do a zillion things at once – and I think, Oh, please go away: I can't deal with this now. But when they are insistent, like Smithy's mum and Kath's first husband, and the mum of the guy I read beside the road, then I have to give in and do a reading. And usually those are the ones who end up having a huge impact on the person receiving them, and they leave me understanding why it is spirit are desperate to use me.

They also leave me thinking how cool spirit are, and how fortunate I am that I can do what I do.

CHAPTER 16

Back to work

The summer break is sacred to me. During the year I spend a big chunk of my time travelling around the country doing shows, and the trips I've made overseas in the past couple of years have meant I've sometimes been away from home for weeks at a time, and I really miss my daughter Jade. So once the final bell of the year rings and school is out, work goes on the backburner so I can hang out with my girl, as well as unwind and try to de-stress a little after everything I've been through during the year.

Once the madness of Christmas and New Year's is over, January is either spent on the water in my boat or on the deck by the pool. I hang out with my daughter and my friends, and I try to switch off as much as possible. I let spirit know: Okay, this is my time now.

Sometimes I do end up doing work that is urgent and important, but usually by the time February rolls around I am pretty chilled out and quite settled into a relaxing routine.

And then I have to go back to work.

I know I'm not alone in finding it hard to switch back into work mode after the summer holidays. And those first couple of shows of the year can certainly require a bit of adjusting, as I go from being a cruisy dad to professional medium.

So in 2019 Gemma thought it would be good to ease me back into work by doing something a bit different. She suggested that instead of going straight into a theatre setting for my first show of the year, we could do an event in a really cool location that would be a bit more laidback. Rather than doing full-on readings the whole time, I could do a guided meditation, have a question-and-answer session, and generally be more casual. And I could also wear shorts, a T-shirt and jandals. Choice!

Nek minute, Gemma had booked a venue – a marquee in the grounds of a retreat in the middle of beautiful bush on Auckland's North Shore – and started advertising the *Closer to Nature* event on my Facebook page. Tickets sold out in an hour, so she organised a second show for the next day.

Suddenly my nice, easy slide back into work didn't seem quite as relaxed as it had, with two full days to do, but even so I was looking forward to doing something a bit different.

The location proved to be lovely, the weather was good, and everyone who turned up seemed to appreciate the relaxed atmosphere. I'm always a bit nervous when I haven't read for a while, as it can take a little while for me to get going. This time it didn't help that unfortunately, as tends to happen at my shows, on the first day there was a problem with the sound system, and we had to muck around trying to sort that out.

Then someone else using the facility decided to start banging in the posts to put up another marquee right next to us, which shattered the peace and quiet just a little bit. Gemma had to go and sort that one out. And the next day somebody else decided to start up a lawnmower right outside, just as I was doing a sensitive reading with a woman who'd lost her mum.

But never mind, these things happen. Once we'd got through the teething problems and I started launching into full-on readings, the nerves went and I was reminded why it is that I love what I do. I had spirit lining up through the door – or rather, through the back flap of the marquee – wanting to talk to their loved ones, and both days I was blown away by many of the messages I was able to pass on. I'd like to share a few of them with you.

Two very different dads

It's interesting the way some readings pan out. The person getting messages from spirit via me may expect to hear from particular people, and then others turn up who completely throw them for a loop.

This happened to a lady called Sharon at the *Closer to Nature* event. She asked me a question about adoption, and I think she may have been hoping her birth mother would show up, so she could ask why she had given her away. But there was no sign of this woman; instead, Sharon's adoptive father, Derek, came through. That was all well and good because he was a lovely man, and it was a nice opportunity for him to tell his daughter how much he loved her. He was a bit nervous to start with, but once he got going it was bang, bang, bang – everything he showed me resonated with Sharon, like the fact that he was a handyman who loved fixing stuff and that things had to be perfectly done.

Derek mentioned that his wife, Alice, who was still on this side of life, was a churchgoer and would be in for a shock when she crossed over. 'It's not what she perceives it to be,' he said to me.

He then asked about some kind of statue or ornament: was it being moved? Sharon gasped when I said that.

'The last gift he bought my mother was a huge cascading fountain. She is in the middle of selling her property, but the fountain will be going with her.'

Throughout the reading, Derek kept repeating how much he loved his daughter and how proud he was of her. I was so happy to pass this message on: if Sharon had any feelings of rejection because she had been given up for adoption by her birth mother, at least she could rest assured that she was deeply loved by her adoptive parents. Of course, she already knew that.

Then I became aware that Derek had brought another man through with him. This guy, George, was the complete opposite to Derek, who had been happily chatting away. He did not want to come anywhere near me; instead, he hung right back until he was just about out of the marquee. He didn't like the fact that I could communicate with spirit, and he was very wary of me. It didn't take me long to figure out why.

George, who turned out to be Sharon's father-in-law, had not been a very nice person when he was on this side of life, and now he'd crossed over he was having to face up to some of the things he had done – or hadn't done – while he was alive.

Unlike Derek, he had never told his kids – including Sharon's husband, Terry – that he loved them or was proud of them. I was being shown that there had been a lot of abuse, both emotional and physical, and Sharon confirmed that, yes, that was the case.

I said to Sharon, 'If you don't mind, I am going to be blunt. This man is as hard as nails. To understand how hard he is, I'm getting that it's not like chopping down a tree, it's like having to saw through a concrete power pole. He's that hard, and he has caused a lot of harm.'

I could see that Terry was suffering because of issues he'd had with this dad. 'There's a lot of sadness and depression, but he doesn't know how to talk about it,' I said. Sharon nodded. 'My heart feels so heavy for him, because your husband is a lovely man but there are unresolved issues with his dad and that man has a lot to answer for.'

No wonder George was hiding around a corner.

Next, I could see alcohol. 'Who is drinking too much?' I asked Sharon. She confirmed it was her husband.

'I can see why. He's trying to run away from his pain.'

What a sad situation. I couldn't get over the contrast between the two dads: one who loved his daughter to bits and made sure she knew that; the other who had caused ongoing damage by being abusive and never telling his son he cared.

But I was also seeing something else. I could tell that now George was in spirit, he had the opportunity to look back on his life and review the way he had been.

'He may not have shown that he loved his kids, but he did, in his way. He knows what he did was wrong, and he is admitting it. He regrets the way he was to his son and his other children, and he is sorry to you, too,' I said to Sharon.

'I can't call him a gentleman, like I can with your dad, because he's not one. Some serious stuff has gone on with him, but now he has the chance to change, and he's doing it. Under all of the stuff that has gone on, there is light inside your father-in-law now.'

I asked Sharon to make sure she told her husband all of that, because he desperately needed to hear it, and she said she would.

I went on to get a couple more family names from George, and then Derek came back, which I was pleased about, because I enjoyed talking to him so much more. He was a real character, and I had to laugh as he went on about making sure the fountain was moved properly when the time came. 'Make sure straps are on it when you lift it!' he instructed me to tell Sharon. He couldn't help himself: he was always the perfectionist.

It was a privilege to talk to Derek, and I was so pleased to be able to tell Sharon: 'Your dad says, "Check this out, I'm not wobbling anymore."'

She gasped. 'He had Parkinson's,' she said.

Well, that's all gone now.

It was important for Sharon to hear from her dad, and to have it confirmed that, while she may have been adopted, she was loved as much as he would have loved her had she been his biological child.

But I think it was even more vital that Derek brought George along with him, so George could say sorry to his son. I'm pretty sure that was one of the most important messages of the day, and something Terry really needed to hear. I hope it has been able to help him.

Sharon says

The reading was amazing; everything Kelvin said meant something to me. It was lovely to hear from my dad, and Kelvin's description of him was spot-on. Dad was a perfectionist and always fixing things. He was very wobbly at the end with the Parkinson's, and kept falling over all the time.

It was bizarre that my father-in-law came through. He was a very hard man, like Kelvin said; a very cruel and abusive man. He hurt all of his kids in one way or another. My husband really suffers because of him, and is having to see a psychologist to try to make sense of it all.

It was quite hard to hear some of what George said, and I am not sure how my husband will take it. But I will tell him.

> My mum is going to be rapt when I tell her about Dad. And we will make sure we are very careful when we move that fountain!

The right thing to do

Imagine living for eight years wondering if you had made the correct decision when it came to whether or not to keep a loved one alive artificially. That's what a guy named Steve, who came along to the second day of my *Closer to Nature* shows, was going through.

He asked me if he had done the right thing by switching off his mum's life-support.

'I still don't know if I made the right decision,' he said. 'I worry about it all the time, and it was eight years ago.'

His mum was with me, and she didn't waste time when it came to answering his question.

'Your mum is saying thank you for doing it. She says, "I was done, there was no point in dragging things on." She wants you to stop beating yourself up because it was ultimately the best thing to do. She wouldn't have wanted to be kept on life-support.'

I could see by the look on his face that it was a huge relief to hear that. His mum, Ann, came across to me as quite a strong and forthright lady, and I got the feeling that if she hadn't been happy about him flicking the switch she would have said so.

Ann went on to tell me a few other things, including the fact that after she died she didn't like the way her hair had been done by the funeral home. But fortunately someone had realised that it wasn't right, and her hair had been done again, properly this time.

'Thank you for changing my hair,' she said. 'It was so much better.'

I could sense that Ann was quite an authoritative person, and Steve confirmed this when he told me that she had been a nurse.

'Yes, I'm getting that matron vibe!' I said. 'She was good at her job, but she was quite hard on herself. She got on and did what was needed, and there was no time to get emotional over how she was able to help people. But I'm pleased to say that now she is in the afterlife, she is getting accolades for what she did in her life. She's absorbing the love and gratitude of the people she nursed.'

Steve's father-in-law also came through, and showed me a paintbrush and a mailbox. That was his way of telling Steve he needed to get on with painting the house, and fix a problem with the mailbox. Steve and his wife, Helena, both had a laugh over that.

It wasn't a long reading, but it was enough to get that all-important message across to Steve from his mum. I was very glad I was able to give him peace of mind.

Steve says

My mum was on life-support after having a heart attack, and the doctors told us there was no brain activity. They had tried all sorts of things, including putting her on a bed of ice, which can reboot the brain. But there was nothing.

My dad couldn't bring himself to make the decision to turn off the machine, and neither could my sister. It was too hard for them. So I made it. And for the past eight years, I have been beating myself up over that. Was it the right thing to do? Should we have kept her on it for longer? It has bothered me every single day.

When Kelvin told me that my mum said thank you, it was

the right thing to do, it was like a huge weight had been lifted. I instantly felt so much better.

The bizarre thing is that the day after my mum died, I was in bed and she suddenly appeared in the room, standing at the end of the bed. It completely freaked me out – I pulled the covers over my head and yelled 'Go away!' It was really scary. I had never experienced anything like that before, and I haven't since. I couldn't help wondering if she was there because I had done the wrong thing in taking her off life-support, and I have been second-guessing myself about it ever since. Now I can let it go.

What Kelvin said about Mum's hair really got to me – that was exactly what happened, but he couldn't have known that. She was very fussy about her hair and used to get it set. When she died the people at the funeral home did it the wrong way, so we made sure it was changed.

The stuff from my father-in-law was also accurate. Our mailbox was in the wrong place, and for a year we got notes from our mailman – we're rural delivery – asking if we could move it so that he didn't have to get out of his van to deliver the mail. That would have annoyed my father-in-law big time. And he wouldn't have been too impressed by the fact I've only half-painted the house.

Everything Kelvin said struck a chord. Even though I had seen my mum that time after she died, I was still in the 'I'm not really sure about this stuff' frame of mind. But after what Kelvin said to me, I'm not anymore.

A formal apology

I seemed to get quite a few readings from mothers in spirit at both of the *Closer to Nature* shows, most of whom were delighted to have the chance to communicate with their children. I could feel the swell of love from many of them, and they wanted me to tell their grown-up children 'I am so proud of you'.

But there was one reading from a mum to a daughter that had a completely different vibe. The reading was for a woman called Carol, whose uncle came through first. Everything was fine, but when Mum showed up, the atmosphere changed, and things became pretty intense.

'Your mum wants to make sure you know that she is sorry, that she realises she could have been more gentle on you.'

I could feel my thumb being pushed down, which is an indication of someone being really firm, and putting pressure on another person.

'She wanted the best from everybody, especially you, and she was really tough on you. Now she's truly sorry, and she wants to formally apologise. She needs to clear the air.'

Carol's mum had come to realise that she had missed out on a relationship with her daughter that could have been so much better if it wasn't for her own difficult behaviour.

'Our bond was not as strong as it should have been, because I was stubborn and arrogant. Today is the day I try to put that right,' her mum said.

I think it takes a lot of courage to admit you've made a mistake and to speak out like that. It was sad that the mum had not been able to do that on this side of life, but at least Carol got to hear it, and to know her mum was genuinely sorry for not being the mum she could, and should, have been.

Carol says

Kelvin was exactly right about my mum. She was very hard on me, although not to start with. As a child, I was a bit of a star. At primary school I was usually top of my class and good at sport. I also did well at boarding school. I was always in the top academic class and often captain of every form class. I represented the school in many sports, including captaining the first XI hockey team. In my final year I was head girl and received the school Colours Cup for Sport. Mum had plenty to skite about. She would say 'Carol is doing this, and Carol is doing that' whenever she met anyone. She was proud of what I achieved.

All of this began to change at the end of my final year at school when I met a boy Mum didn't like. (It was mutual, he used to call her 'The Dragon'.) I was quite strong-minded, but I had met my match. He refused to take no for an answer – with everything. I did try to break up with him, but I was not strong enough.

I ended up getting pregnant, and that's when Mum really turned on me. She told me she was ashamed of me and that I had ruined her life. It was the 1960s, and getting pregnant when you weren't married was considered a terrible sin. Three weeks after finding out I was pregnant I married my boyfriend. I made my own wedding dress, which caused a huge battle with Mum. She said I couldn't wear white because I was a sinner, but I held my ground and won. My wedding dress was white.

Things didn't improve after my baby was born. Every time I spoke to my mother, she would say things like 'I saw so-and-so in the street today, but I had to cross to the other side of the road because I didn't want to be asked about you, I'm so ashamed.'

After putting up with this behaviour for two years, I finally said to her: 'Mum, if you don't shut up and stop saying these thing, you will never see me and the baby again.' To her credit, she did stop, but was still always critical of me. It was always about Mum and her needs, and never about me. She had no concept of, or empathy for, how depressed and unhappy I was in my abusive marriage.

After five years with my husband I hit rock bottom, and was in such a bad way that doctors had booked me into the mental health ward at Auckland Hospital. I was suicidal, but someone must have been looking after me, because on the very day I was due to be admitted to hospital I started work as a teacher aide at a local primary school. That was thanks to my mother-in-law's best friend, who offered me the job, and it literally saved my life. At last I felt I had some worth and had something of merit to give. I wasn't as useless as I had constantly been told. However, it took me another five years to get out of my marriage.

Two weeks after I turned 40 I started the first of many personal growth courses. My life gradually improved as I began to understand why I had attracted all of these challenging events (including a second failed marriage). Sadly, once again my mother did not understand, and her response to all my efforts to heal myself was to say 'Aren't you fixed yet?'

For many years I was sad that my mother was never there for me, but as my awareness grew, I started to look more closely at her and realised she never looked really happy. Her smile never reached her eyes.

> I had always thought this was because she had been brought up in a household where her father was abusive to her mother. After Mum died, I saw a clairvoyant and Mum came through. At the end of the reading the clairvoyant said, 'I don't think your grandmother was the only one violently abused by your grandfather.' Now it all made perfect sense. If it was true that my mum had been abused as a child, and I suspect it was, then that explained why she was never able to be there for me because, unlike me, she had never had the opportunity to heal from her shame and hurt.
>
> Although I had been able to make my peace with Mum before she died, for her to come through to Kelvin and to offer me a formal apology through him in front of other people was very special. I do believe she is sorry, and it was good to hear her say that.

Mum knows best

In a somewhat less intense reading, I had a mum come through in spirit who read the riot act to her daughter about her diet, and lectured her about eating rubbish food. This lady in spirit was a great cook who had loved feeding people, and throughout the reading I kept seeing food, including soup and shortbread. Luckily I'd just had lunch, or my mouth would have been watering.

She also started showing me expensive-looking jewellery, including a sparkling diamond ring. It soon became apparent that she was unhappy about the arguments over the distribution of her jewellery following her death. Her daughter confirmed that there had been a dispute in the family over the jewellery, with legal action being taken.

'She always said that if her will was contested she would come back and haunt the people involved,' the daughter said.

I could imagine her mum doing that!

The lady in spirit also mentioned that she had somebody with her whose death had been a fatality – that was the word I heard, 'fatality'. When I asked her how they died she wouldn't tell me. 'It's happened, there's no point in dwelling on it. Just let my daughter know they're here and I am taking care of them.'

It turned out that the daughter's fiancé had been killed in a hit-and-run accident many years earlier, and she had always wondered if it was deliberate. Mum clearly wasn't prepared to go down that path, and she didn't tell me anything else. The other person she mentioned who was with her did not come through, but if it was her daughter's fiancé, at least she knows he's with her mum on the other side.

Another mum came through who wanted to thank her daughter for the amazing job she did of looking after her in her final days. This lady in spirit was very cool, with a big personality – when I asked her if she could step forward so I could get information from her more easily she said, 'Don't boss me around!'

She had very strong energy, and she welcomed the chance to say thank you. While I was passing on the message to her daughter, it suddenly became apparent that this mum in spirit had another daughter who was in the audience with her husband. As it turned out, I happened to be acquainted with this couple, Mike and Julie, but I had no idea of the connection when I started doing the reading – the sisters weren't sitting next to each other.

I never normally read for people I know, but I knew the mum really wanted to keep going with her messages. So I explained to the audience: 'I do actually know Mike and Rachel – I mean Mike and Julie. Sorry, I don't know where the name Rachel came from.'

The sister I'd never met before piped up: 'I'm Rachel.'

Okay then, Mum must have given me that name. 'Right, hello Rachel!'

A whole load of information came through, including the fact that Mum had had cancer. She said there was somebody else she needed to bring forward, and it was a person who had been taken away without anyone knowing the reason why. Those were her exact words. She said she had them in her arms, and she wanted to let her family know that this person was safe. 'He's in the light,' she said to me. 'He's being looked after.'

I wasn't sure how he fitted into the scheme of things to start with, but then I could tell by the reaction from Mike and Julie that these words had a huge impact on them, and it became clear that this soul was their boy.

The thing is, under normal circumstances I would never have been able to give them this message because, as I say, I don't read for people I know at my shows. But spirit knew I needed to tell them about him being safe, so they went around the houses by initiating a reading with the sister, Rachel, who was a stranger to me.

I was able to give Mike and Julie some beautiful messages from this young guy – including him telling his dad that he was with him whenever he went fishing – and I think it made a difference.

It certainly reinforced to me that we should never underestimate spirit. They're clever, they're determined, and if they really, really want to get in touch, they'll find a way.

CHAPTER 17

Dealing with sudden death

In my line of work, I deal constantly with people who are bereaved, and I see many different forms of grief.

I see people who are incredibly stoic and accepting of what has happened to the person they lost. I see those who are angry – often they feel cheated or they are furious at someone they consider to be responsible for their loved one's death. And I see those who are so broken by loss that they are barely holding it together.

How we respond to death can depend on a variety of factors, including our relationship with that person, how young or old they were when they passed, and the circumstances surrounding their death.

It's understandable that you're likely to find it harder to deal with the death of a child whose time on this Earth has been cut short, than with the passing of a grandparent or older adult who has lived a long and satisfying life. But having said that, I've had a teenage girl sobbing her heart out at one of my shows because she was so cut up over losing her grandad, who meant the world to her. She was devastated not to have had more time with him.

How your loved one died can also affect how well you cope with their loss. It is awful when someone is consumed by a horrible illness, and you have to watch them suffering as their life ebbs away in front of you. When the inevitable happens, the pain is still overwhelming, even though you knew what was coming. But it can help if knowing they were dying meant you got to have some quality time together, along with some important conversations and the chance to say things that needed to be said.

You don't get to do that when your loved one dies suddenly and unexpectedly. What often makes those kinds of deaths so very hard to deal with is the shock. How can it be possible that someone was just there, living life as normal, and now they are gone, their life snuffed out? If the death was violent or brutal in any way, that can make things even worse.

I often see how the shock of a sudden and unexpected death can make grief even more painful to bear, and the passing of a loved one harder to accept. I see people who are still reeling from the shock even though it's many years since that special person died. They're not only dealing with that big gaping hole in their lives, but the horror of how their loved one went. Those readings can be really intense and hard for me to do, because not only is the person in the audience still in shock, but the one in spirit can be too.

When spirit are in shock

'Holy shit!' I yelled at the top of my voice. 'What's going on?'

Actually, it wasn't me yelling, it was the guy in spirit who'd turned up. 'Why am I here?' he shouted, via me. He was really freaking out.

'It's okay, calm down,' I said.

He turned to his grandfather, who was also in spirit and had brought him through from the other side. 'Grandad, what's happening?'

What was happening was that this young man had come through during a reading I was doing with this very cool older bloke. There was a group of this man's family in the audience, including his wife, daughter, two grandsons and a granddaughter. The family were happy to see him, but I got the feeling they were anxious to talk to someone else. And then I realised Grandad had somebody with him, a younger soul.

At first I thought this other soul was a child, because of the way he had been brought through by an older family member, and because Grandad was super-protective of him. Grandad still thought of him as a young lad who he needed to look after and I was picking up on this.

Because he was hanging back I couldn't see him, I could only feel his energy. But something didn't seem quite right, and I realised that actually he was not a child, he was older. When he moved forward it immediately became obvious that he was probably in his twenties.

When I started talking directly to the guy in spirit, he lost it. It wasn't just the fact that I could see and talk to him that was blowing his mind; he was still reeling over being dead. I found out later that it had only been four months since he'd died in a car accident.

I don't normally yell and swear like that, and I am sure I made a few people jump, but that was his response to me talking to him.

I explained to his family: 'The reason he is so stressed is that he doesn't really understand what happened. He was here one minute and gone the next. He is trying to be as calm as possible, but he can't believe I can see him.'

I got him to calm down a little, and he said to me, 'I was taken away tragically and I am still in as much shock as my family are.'

Once he got used to the idea that I could see him and pass on messages to his whānau, the first thing he wanted me to do was let them know that Grandad was looking after him. He mentioned that somebody in the family needed to go easy on smoking weed. 'Knock it off, it's not helping,' he said.

He mentioned he had good guns, as in biceps, and I got the feeling he was inclined to be a bit vain. He liked to chat to the ladies.

Now that he had calmed down, I could tell that he was a really hard-case guy. He was witty and funny and really popular, one of those guys everyone loved.

It was important for him to let his family know that he was safe with his pop and they weren't to worry about him – he wasn't alone. But he was finding it hard to come to terms with the fact that he didn't get to say goodbye to anyone.

He mentioned his funeral, and how much he'd loved it. 'It was magic,' he said. His mum said later that his coffin had been transported on a Big Mack truck, and more than 800 people had turned up. 'He didn't realise how much he was loved, he was quite overcome,' I told the family.

He showed me that his brother spoke at his funeral, which he knew was hard for him, but he had appreciated what his brother had said. 'He was standing next to you, and what you said was amazing. He loves you, too, bro.'

He really wanted to make sure that his brother was not consumed with grief. 'Don't give up on your life because I'm not there. You have to live.'

I could hear him saying 'twins', so I asked where the twins were in the family. It turned out that he and his bro were born 15 months apart, and were as close as twins. His mum said they had celebrated their twenty-first birthdays together.

While his time on Earth had been cut short, and that had been a big shock, he wanted his family to know that he'd had an incredible life. He'd had his ups and downs and troubles, but he'd had wonderful times, too.

I felt the need to explain to his whānau why some of us leave earlier than others. I talked about how, before we actually get here, we sit down with our Creator when our soul is created, and we decide what journeys we need to go on to get the experience necessary to gain our angel's wings. We also choose the people we are going to be with for that journey.

'Whatever we've chosen to happen to us – and that can include dying early in an accident – is because our souls need to evolve. You don't get your wings without having experiences.

'We may have to come back to this side of life many times to get our wings, after which time we can stay in heaven – or home, as I call it.

'I know you are feeling ripped off, and I know it sounds hard that he would choose this, but he chose you to be his family because he knew he would have a great life with you, and he also knew you would cope with this. He knew everything was a risk, and he was prepared to take it. Unfortunately, the incident that took his life was the way that he chose to leave in order for him to gain his experiences. Do not feel responsible for that – it was his choice before he even got here to begin this life.'

I hoped that was making sense to them; I know that it can be difficult for people to grasp this concept sometimes. And then there was something else I knew I needed to explain to them.

'If anyone is feeling low because of his passing and doesn't want to be here, there's no way he is going to let you do anything stupid.

You wouldn't end up with him anyway, you'd end up in a different place.'

I sounded like I was giving a lecture, but it needed to be said. 'I know how low people can get when they lose someone they love, but he's going "No way, you've got your own pathways to go down, you've got a vibrant future ahead of you guys."'

By the time I finished the reading he was a lot calmer and had accepted what had happened to him. He wanted me to make sure his family knew how much he loved them, and to thank them for being part of his experience.

His mum said later that she wished she'd asked me to tell him how much she loved and missed him. But she didn't need to. Trust me, Mum, he knows.

A horrific experience

Feeling the pain that someone now in spirit experienced when they died is part and parcel of my job. Usually it's quick – perhaps a fleeting chest pain if the person had a heart attack or a brief stinging sensation if they were stabbed. I get enough so I know what happened, and then thankfully it passes.

But that wasn't the case with a reading I did during the *Legacy Tour* with TJ. A guy came through for me, and I could tell that he had died in an accident. All of a sudden I felt like I was being choked. I started coughing and I couldn't breathe or speak. It was horrific – I actually felt like I had had half my head ripped off. It was so bad I had to walk off stage and leave TJ to it while I did my best to recover. Eventually the sensation passed, but while it lasted it was probably one of the most horrific physical responses I have ever had to doing a reading.

It turned out the guy in spirit had died in a boating accident and suffered terrible injuries to his head. He was distressed about what had happened to him, which was totally understandable. But he was also upset because the woman in the audience who was connected to him had previously been given a message to pass on to his wife and she hadn't done it. I think the reason I went through such a physical response was because he really wanted the reading to have an impact on the person in the audience, and to make sure this woman told his wife that after going through the horrible accident he was now okay. I'm betting that after that display from me, which might have looked like I was about to check out then and there, she did as she was asked.

With about 90 percent of the readings I do, the people in spirit have the same initial message they want to pass on. After 'I love you and I miss you', it's 'please don't worry about me, I'm okay'.

People like this guy who have passed suddenly in accidents seem particularly keen to get that message across. They can tell that their loved ones are worried sick that they suffered, and they want them to stop fretting. They get how hard it is for their family members to move through the grieving process when they are obsessed with the manner of the death. They want you to let it go.

Often with accidents, the people left behind have trouble adjusting to the fact that the event that killed their loved one was a random thing, and a case of apparently being in the wrong place at the wrong time.

Sometimes people try to apportion blame – was it really an accident or is someone responsible for what happened? I had this during a reading with a woman who lost a dear friend in a fall. She was convinced foul play must have been involved because surely her mate couldn't have just tripped and fallen to her death. That was too random, too freaky.

Well, sadly, these things do happen, and again, it helps if you understand that dying that way is part of that person's journey.

From slumped to smiling

A young woman whose partner had only recently died in a car crash was understandably emotional as I read for her. She was in pieces over losing him – they were planning a future together and it was a horrendous shock for him to be there one minute and gone the next. It didn't help that she'd had to identify his body as none of his family was around to do it. She was still struggling to accept that he had gone, and when he came through for her, she was slumped in her seat, her head down and her aura incredibly dark, like a big black cloud hanging over her.

This guy in spirit told me how they were planning to build a life together, but said she had to accept that he wasn't there and she would have to move on without him. He told me to tell her that she would be a mother one day, and she would be an amazing one. He also said she had the choice of different paths to follow, and everything would be okay for her.

He was very cheeky, her bloke, and he went on about how gorgeous he was. It was lovely to see the effect that hearing from him had on her. By the end of the reading she was sitting up tall in her seat and smiling.

Afterwards she got talking to my PA Crystal, who gave her a copy of my book *Soul Secrets*. It contains advice and affirmations on everything from dealing with grief to learning to be as positive as possible. The idea behind it is to inspire people to lead a happier and more fulfilling life. Crystal told me later that it was a real thrill for her to watch this young woman flicking through the book and the smile on her face growing wider as she read my words. 'I really think the message that she got tonight will help her with her grieving, and to understand what has happened to her partner,' Crystal said. 'Way to go, KC.'

I hope that my words can help if you're going through loss like this. You can't change what has happened and you can't bring them back, but if you understand that they're not gone, they're just in another dimension and the love between you still exists, then your grief may be a little easier to handle.

CHAPTER 18

Lose the luggage

It happens quite a lot. I'll be doing a show, and chatting away about spirit and life in general in between readings, when I find myself thinking, 'KC, what the hell are you talking about?' Words will come spilling out of my mouth and I have no idea what I am saying or why. I'm left thinking, 'Where is this coming from?'

Of course I know the answer to that: spirit is responsible. Often they will decide that I need to tackle a certain topic and off I go, with no clue what will come out of my mouth next.

The subject might be anything from standing up for yourself through to managing anger. As I address the audience, I know that this message is being given to me because while most of the people there could probably benefit from the advice, there will be a handful of people who really, really need to hear the point I am making. Spirit might even be targeting one person in particular with the words they are getting me to say.

More often than not I will end up doing a reading later on and the person I talk to will say, 'Wow, KC, that message you gave everyone just now really resonates with me. I feel like I was meant to be here to hear what you've said.' Bingo, that's why I came out with it.

At one of my shows, I came back on stage after the half-time break and immediately found myself talking about suitcases, of all things.

'Imagine that everywhere you go you have to lug around two suitcases with you. Each suitcase is full of rocks, and it doesn't matter if you are going to work, to the supermarket, to pick the kids up from school, to the kitchen to cook dinner – you have to have them with you all the time. Imagine how heavy they must be, and how much damage they must be doing to you. They'll break you, right?'

Quite a few people nodded in response.

'Such a stupid thing to do, isn't it, carrying around cases full of rocks that are of no use to you when at the end of the day all you are going to do is hurt yourself? Why would you do that? The thing is, this is exactly what a lot of you here tonight *are* doing. You are carrying around luggage that isn't yours. This luggage is other people's crap, it's their toxic behaviour, their abuse, it's the rubbish they have put you through over the years, and it is weighing you down. When you are abused or treated badly, you can end up carrying this around with you, like a couple of heavy suitcases, and sometimes it is so bad you can't even lift the cases, you have to drag them.

'You did not do anything to deserve this, this is somebody else's selfish agenda, but it is going to harm you. So put the suitcases down, and walk away from them. Do this for yourself.'

The venue went incredibly quiet as I said this. You could have heard a pin drop. 'It's not my job to lecture, but wairua make me say these things. I'm sorry, but there are people in the room tonight who need to hear this.'

I took a deep breath after that and moved on to my next reading. I hoped that whoever needed to hear that message had taken what I needed to say on board. And not long afterwards, I started reading for a woman who I believe the message was directly aimed at.

A tragic loss

I could see one of those roadside crosses, which indicated that the young man in spirit who'd shown up during a reading I was doing with a group of people had died in an accident.

'Who has lost a young person in a crash?' I asked the group. The microphone was passed to a woman called Catherine. She was sat right at the back of the venue so I couldn't really see her, but as soon as I heard her voice her son, who I later found out was called Kent, came through loud and clear.

I could tell he wasn't very old, and it turned out that he had been 16 when he was killed in a car crash 16 years earlier.

I instantly liked this kid. He was cheeky. 'Is that a bar over there?' he said to me. 'I wouldn't mind a beer. Wouldn't mind a doobie either.'

I could see that he was a very handsome young man, with a stunning smile. He acknowledged that there had been a separation between his mum and his dad, and he wouldn't stop going on about how much he loved his mother.

'You're an amazing mum,' he said to Catherine. 'I miss you terribly, and I am so sorry I put you through hell. Please stop worrying about me, I'm okay. I'm having fun over here with my bros. There are lots of old people here, too; they're not so much fun.

But honestly, I'm okay.'

He talked about someone in the family getting a tattoo on his behalf, and Catherine confirmed that her daughter had had Kent's name tattooed on her arm just a couple of weeks earlier. 'I love it,' Kent told me.

Next he mentioned the name Steven, who turned out to be his toddler nephew.

'He wishes he could be here to physically hold Steven in his arms,' I said, feeling Kent's sorrow at not being around for his nephew. 'He's getting quite emotional.'

From what Kent was showing me, I reckoned that Steven might be able to see his uncle. 'When this little fella starts looking over your shoulder and giggling at apparently nothing, he's actually looking at his uncle. When he's old enough to understand, make sure he knows that his uncle is his angel.'

Kent then showed me something really random. 'Does Steven's mother tuck him into bed really tightly? Does she make the bed like a hospital one? Poor kid, he feels like a mummy in those sheets. You might want to tell her to relax on that.'

Kent was really opening up to me, and I liked how funny he was. He had a tendency to use bad language, but not in an abusive or rude way; even so, I was having to edit out the four-letter words as I passed on his messages.

'Does he have a potty mouth?' I asked Catherine.

'Oh yes,' she laughed.

'He's saying, "Don't f***ing rush me, this is my time with my mum."'

He might have been telling me off, but it felt like he trusted me. He definitely preferred me to other mediums his mum had seen. 'You've been to see other spooks, but I didn't like them,' he said to his mum. 'That's why I was a bit weird with them. They thought they had me, but they didn't.'

I could tell that he and I had clicked because we liked the same music. Wairua have to like you to talk to you, and I knew that he thought I was okay, which was why he was being so open and chatty.

The reading had been quite light-hearted because of his jokey personality, but then it suddenly got serious. He needed to tell his mum something important.

'Your son felt ripped off by dying when he did,' I told Catherine. 'That feeling has left him now, but it has stuck with you for all this time. Today, Mum, is the day you have to let that end. He can't change what happened, and he is sick and tired of seeing you struggling. He's saying, "I'm done, Mum, I'm done."'

He wanted her to stop being so sad. He also wanted her to make some other major changes in her life. And this was when I realised why I had been going on about suitcases and carrying other people's luggage earlier.

'He just referred to the story I told about the suitcases, and said, "Well, my mum's not just carrying two suitcases, she's lugging around something much bigger."' I could see the image of two large objects in my mind, and for a moment I was lost for words. 'Help me out,' I said to Kent. 'What are those things called?' He couldn't remember either, and for a moment or two I stood on stage racking my brains over the name of these very common things that I could very clearly see in my third eye.

Finally, it came to me. 'Shipping containers! That's it! You are carrying around so much crap, it's not in suitcases, it's in two shipping containers with handles. That's how much you have to deal with.'

'Actually,' said Catherine, 'I have two shipping containers on my property.'

Okay, then. The shipping containers were not an analogy, they were literal. But how freaky was that? How many people have shipping containers in their garden?

'He says he wants to take those containers full of hurt away from you,' I continued. 'Sweetheart, you have had a very hard life, and today is the day you start fresh. He's showing me that he has taken those containers of pain away.'

There was more her son wanted to share, and he wasn't mincing his words: 'Do not walk among negative people. Do not allow selfish, manipulative, abusive people into your life. I'm taking away your pain, and this doesn't happen again, Mum.'

'I know exactly what he means,' Catherine replied, and I could hear the emotion in her voice.

Kent told his mum to light a candle every day, to bring love and light and joy and comfort into her life. And as he lugged those containers away, he said, 'These are bloody heavy!'

I then went to someone else in the room to answer a question, but I knew I hadn't quite finished with Catherine. Eventually I went back to her.

'My people are telling me that you are a bloody amazing human being,' I said. 'I have to tell you to please believe in yourself. There is something very special about you – you have done so much for other people, and that is great. But there are people who do not deserve your time. Cut them loose, please. Let them go with honour and love. Believe in yourself, and keep up the good work. You are amazing.'

The words came rushing out in a torrent, but I knew I had to say them. Catherine needed to hear those words from me as well as from her son, and she needed to walk free of the crap that had been dragging her down.

No wonder I had gone on about suitcases earlier! For Catherine, it was a crucial message. I hope that other people in the audience that night were able to let go of any baggage they had been lugging around, too.

Catherine says

I really didn't expect Kent would come through for me. But as soon as Kelvin started talking about him, I knew it was my son. Kent was very handsome, he was a happy person, he smoked dope. Kelvin's description was just perfect. And I couldn't believe it when he mentioned the shipping containers!

And I have felt ripped off, that's so true. My heart is so connected to Kent, and it felt like it was ripped out when he died. I can remember every detail from the day he died, what I was wearing when I found out, what was said.

He was the backseat passenger in a car that was in an accident and broke in half. He was wearing a seatbelt, but he suffered terrible injuries and died instantly. The other two people in the car walked away without a scratch.

After Kent died I went from being an outgoing person who was friends with everyone to a hermit. I didn't want to talk to anyone. I had to be there for my two other children, and I went on to adopt another child, but there was such a big gap where Kent had been.

Kelvin was right: I have had a very hard life, with losing Kent, and with other things that have happened to me as well. When he said I had to stay away from manipulative and selfish people, I knew exactly who he meant. I felt like I'd been carrying around baggage because of one particularly toxic situation that really upset me. I have been in a very bad place: in fact, I had been so depressed that I had to get mental health help a couple of weeks before I went to Kelvin's show. I wanted to drive my car into a power pole.

It was interesting that Kelvin used the words 'I'm done',

> because that is what I kept saying to myself: I'm done. I've had enough. But now I feel like Kelvin saved my life. I know Kent doesn't want to see me suffering. I can't keep feeling pain. When Kelvin said to me that I was amazing . . . I have always tried to do things for other people. To hear him say those things about me was awesome. It was what I needed to hear. It has helped me hugely, and I don't doubt for a minute that it all came from Kent.

Time to start living again

It was incredible for me to hear how much my reading with her son had helped Catherine. It's why I do what I do.

I could tell that she had really been through the wringer and that she needed a good helping of self-belief. Catherine's friend Kelly was at my show with her, and she agreed that it was important for her mate to hear what a special person she is.

'Her friends have been telling her that for years, but she doesn't believe it,' Kelly said. 'I hope she will believe it now.'

Kelly said Catherine was always doing things for others, even when she was struggling. 'She put herself out there on Facebook and talked about what she has been through. People have confided in her and they know she understands.'

Kelly remembers Kent as being very protective of his mother, so she's not surprised that he tried to help her.

'I was a bit sceptical about coming along, I have to admit, but everything that was said was so accurate, and it was just beautiful to hear. Catherine has been through a really terrible time, and I hope that she is now able to start living again.'

I hope so, too – it's what her boy wants for his awesome mum.

CHAPTER 19

I can feel the love tonight

One of the worst parts of my job is that I can feel what spirit feel. If they died of a heart attack, I will often feel a pain in my chest. If they had asthma, I will struggle to breathe. If they took their own life because they were despondent over the break-up of a relationship, that sorrow will hit me hard.

But while this can be a negative, there is also a positive side. One of the best parts of my job is also that I can feel what spirit feel. That means I can feel the joy they experience because their wife chats to their picture every night before she goes to bed and tells them about her day. I want to burst with the pride they are experiencing because they are delighted to see their kids growing into happy, healthy, successful young people. I can also feel the love that spirit has for those still on this side of life, and in some cases it is absolutely beautiful.

As someone who has not had a lot of success in the relationships stakes – the less said about that, the better – I love it when I get to pass on messages from someone in spirit to a person in the audience they adore. It is such a wonderful, warm emotion, although it is often bittersweet because they miss the person so much. But by letting me feel their emotions, they give me a glimpse of what it feels like to have a true, sweet love – and, man, that's awesome!

And while it is exciting to feel the thrill of young love, there's something really special about the love between an older couple, whose feelings for each other have gone through lots of ups and downs and stood the test of time. That love, which might have existed for 40, 50 or 60 years on this side of life, doesn't diminish when one of them passes away. The husband or wife may not be with them physically anymore, but their love is just the same.

It's always so nice to read for an elderly person and connect to their sweetheart. Call me soppy, but it makes me want to cry. And I do, quite often!

A night for romance

Sometimes my shows seem to take on a bit of a theme. One might be all about mums lecturing their kids, another might focus on people needing to forgive one another and accept their differences.

I was about halfway through a show in Pukekohe, near Auckland, when I realised love and romance appeared to be the theme of the night. I was getting lots of warm feelings reading for couples who had spent a long time together, and who missed each other terribly. It was very special.

The first reading was for a woman who was there with her daughter.

'Where is the connection to Margaret?' I asked. 'Or Marge?'

'I'm Marjorie,' she said.

'Well, Marjorie, your husband is here and what a lovely man he is. He's blowing kisses to his girls. Oh man, he's so happy to be here and to be seeing you. He loves you so much.'

Her husband, whose name was Ernie, had been so desperate to connect with her that he had even put aside his doubts about people like me who can make that happen.

'He's telling me he didn't really understand all this medium stuff when he was alive, and he still didn't really get it once he was living in spirit. But he wanted to see you so much that he asked upstairs – and by that, I mean the angels – how he could tell his wife he loved her, just one more time. They told him to go and see KC. So he's been hanging around, trying to get me to find you. There are things he needs to tell you.'

Marjorie confirmed that Ernie, who she had been married to for nearly 60 years, wasn't the kind of person who believed in mediums and communicating with spirit. 'He would have said to me, "If you want to go to something like that, go, but I'm not coming with you."'

But now he was beyond happy that I could put him in touch with his beloved wife. By this point, the tears were starting to roll down my face, I was so overcome with Ernie's emotion.

'I had the best life with my darling wife,' he told me. 'My love for her is huge, and I miss her so much. I miss my best friend.'

When spirit want to show me that the love they have shared with someone was massive, I often get an image of Rose and Jack (played by Kate Winslet and Leonardo DiCaprio) from the movie *Titanic*. When my third eye shows me the two of them on the bow of the ship with their arms outstretched, I know whoever I'm reading for has also had an epic love – and I was getting that with Marjorie and Ernie.

To prove to her that it really was him, Ernie gave me a few details, including the fact that he had done it rough before he passed.

'He's really opinionated about doctors, isn't he?' I said to Marjorie. 'He's really nutting off. He says they don't know what they are doing – one minute they tell you this, the next it's something else. They took something away – did he have surgery?'

Marjorie said yes, he had surgery, and he had got frustrated with the doctors who were treating him.

'He wants me to tell you, look love, I am not suffering anymore. I am feeling fantastic. I was scared of dying, of leaving my wife and my family. But I am not scared anymore.'

Ernie showed me that he was a keen gardener who used to take a knife to go and dig the weeds out of his lawn. 'The lawns haven't been the same since I left,' he said, sounding a tiny bit disappointed.

Marjorie said he loved his garden, and unfortunately she couldn't do the amount of work he used to do.

'This might sound crazy, but is there a statue in the garden that has been moved?'

Marjorie had to own up to that. 'We had a statue of an eighteenth-century girl with a basket; we called her Phoebe. He was quite proud of it sitting on the bank in the garden, but after he died I moved it down the back by the clothesline.'

'Ah, you've been busted!' I laughed. 'He knows!'

Ernie then had a message for his daughter, Judith. 'Thanks so much for looking after Mum. Please know that you can't always fix everything for someone else who might lose their spark after they lose someone they love. You have to let them ride the waves and be there when they need you. He's very grateful you've done that for Mum.'

I could sense Ernie was a really nice guy with a heart of gold, the sort who would do anything for anyone, and Marjorie confirmed yes, he was a true gentleman.

As the reading was starting to wind up, I could tell Ernie really didn't want to go.

'He doesn't want to say goodbye to you; he had to do that before and he doesn't want to do it again. Sweetheart, your husband will be waiting for you and while he's excited about being with you again one day, he says you've got a lot more to do here before you come over.

'He's not going to say goodbye, he's going to say "Until we meet again".'

But even when I had moved on to someone else, Ernie was still there, lurking by the curtain. He called out to me, 'Thank you so much, KC, for doing this!'

In all the readings I have done over the years, I don't think I have ever had anyone in spirit try so hard to get to their loved one. I'm just glad I could help out.

Ernie, it was my pleasure.

Glowing with love

A reading I moved on to not long after the one for Ernie and Marjorie felt very similar to start with. Once again I was reading for a mum and a daughter, and Dad was coming through, desperate to tell his wife how much he loved her and missed her. I found out later that, just like Ernie and Marjorie, this couple had been married for nearly 60 years, too.

And, like Ernie, this guy in spirit, whose name was Keith, wasn't quite sure how this business of using me to communicate with his family worked.

Initially two other blokes came through first: a guy called Joe who passed of cancer and a younger guy who died tragically. It turned out that Keith had had a workmate called Michael who had drowned.

And then Keith was there, yelling 'I love you! I love you!' to his wife, Ann. Man, was he happy to see her and their daughter Michelle. They were sat close to the front, and I could see that Ann had a very dark aura. It turned out that it had only been three months since Keith had died, and she was still utterly grief-stricken.

Keith showed me that he'd had a heart attack, and said he died instantly. 'Nothing could have been done,' he told me.

Keith didn't dwell on the negatives, and turned out to be a bit of a joker. He said the heart attack was down to 'all that good tucker my wife fed me'. He didn't want to be morbid – 'Bugger that!' he said – so he was trying to be funny. But he was also a bit nervous to start with, because all he wanted to do was give Ann a hug, and he couldn't. His love for her was off the charts.

Keith mentioned a family member in Australia, and it turned out he had a son there. 'You need to tell him you went to the spooky guy's show and talked to me,' I instructed her. 'Dad is watching out for him and is very proud.'

Keith showed me that he had been popular down at the Cossie Club or RSA, and had quite a few mates. There was a huge turnout to his funeral, he said.

Then I could see teeth. 'Did he have some teeth missing? He says they are all there now.'

Ann explained, 'He lost so much weight that his false teeth kept falling down, so I took them out. After he died I gave them to the funeral director and said, "Please put them in – he wouldn't want to go without his teeth."'

Keith showed me that he had been unwell for some time before he died, but in the end he went quickly from a heart attack, which his family confirmed.

'He was pleased it ended that way. He was over being sick and seeing you guys hurting so much. He really loves his family.'

Keith went on to talk about his family members, including a child who was going to have a few issues. 'He's going to come off the rails a bit and everyone will freak out, but don't worry: Grandad is going to steer him into the light. Just give him time to do that.'

He joked about the fact that Ann had a tonne of knick-knacks in the house. 'How am I supposed to get into the house to talk to you, they are everywhere!' So if Ann's ornaments start randomly falling off shelves, it'll be Keith to blame.

There was more he wanted to say about Ann and how much he loved her, but he was the kind of person who kept his feelings close to his chest and he didn't want to go into too much detail in front of so many other people.

But he was determined to give her a bit of a lecture.

'Stop fretting because of what happened, my darling,' he said. 'Nothing can change it. I am upset that I have left you, but you need to stop being so sad. I am tired of seeing you crying: I want you to be the fun-loving woman I fell in love with. I feel like I need to give you a kick in the bum to tell you to get on with life, keep living it. You have beautiful grandchildren – be around for them. Stop isolating yourself and enjoy your life again. Please.'

As the reading began wrapping up, Keith couldn't resist one last attempt at making his wife laugh. He told me: 'I'd really like to nibble on my wife's ear, because I haven't done that for a while, but I guess it is a bit inappropriate.' What a crack-up!

They, too, had shared a wonderful love, and I was so happy I had been able to bring Keith through for Ann. I was delighted to see that by the end of the reading she looked totally different. Her aura, which had been so dark and filled with sorrow, had changed in front of me, and by the end she was glowing again, which was lovely to see.

Ann says

Keith and I had a wonderful marriage. I first met him when I was 11, when my cousin married his brother. We met again when I was 13, and were together from then on. We got married when I was 19 and had four children, and I keep growling him for the fact that we were a week off celebrating our sixtieth wedding anniversary when he died.

Keith had not been well for a long time. He had cancer, but he had also had two massive heart attacks. The night before he passed away we went to bed about 9.30 p.m. I woke at midnight to find he had his feet sticking out of bed because he said he was hot. I tucked him back in and gave him a kiss. As I got back into bed he grabbed my hand, and then we both fell asleep.

I don't know what woke me at one o'clock, but he had gone. We were still holding hands.

Keith was funny, like Kelvin said. He had a dry sense of humour, and he was very popular, not only at the Cossie Club but also at the bowling club and the rugby club. We had his funeral at the rugby club, and there were over 250 people.

The son he mentioned in Australia, Richard, is very psychic himself. And I do have lots of knick-knacks in my house – my daughter buys them for me. As for Keith wanting to nibble on my ear – that would be him. He was very affectionate.

I'm not surprised my aura was dark. I can't stop crying; I miss Keith so much. It's hard not having him here. Night-time is the hardest, being on my own. But what Kelvin had to say has given me a lot of comfort and I think it is going to make a difference to me.

Overwhelmed by love

The feelings of strong and enduring love continued with another reading I did that night, when I connected with the spirit of a man whose wife, two daughters and granddaughter were in the audience.

It was because of the granddaughter, Christina, that this man, Peter, came through. Christina asked a question about seeing spirit, and as I answered it for her I became aware of someone standing beside me. I could immediately sense how much he missed his family, and how happy he was to see the four women there. He had a message for each of them, but first of all he wanted me to let his wife, Carolyn, know how he felt.

'He wants to tell you he loves you heaps,' I said to her. 'He is struggling without you, to be honest; he feels like he can't breathe without you. There is so much love.'

I couldn't even look at Carolyn because I knew I would cry if I did. It really was an overwhelming sensation.

Peter had messages to pass on to other members of the family. He told me to tell Christina, who was planning to head off to university, that he would help her through her studies. 'He'll carry you through, he'll help you to meet the right people and he will bring love to you,' I told her. 'When that boy turns up who is the right one for you, it will be because of your pop, and he will make sure that boy loves you the way he loves his wife.'

Poor Christina, it was all a bit much for her, and hearing that made her sob out loud. She had obviously been very close to her grandfather. 'Life is going to be full of joyful things for you, my darling, and just because your pop is not there with you physically does not mean he is not there loving and protecting you. He will set things up for you because you deserve the best.'

To Christina's mum (and Carolyn's daughter), Fiona, he mentioned someone with a missing or damaged digit, which turned out to be her husband, who had a toe out of place after it had been run over by a car and crushed. He loved his son-in-law like he was his own son. 'He misses the banter they shared,' I told her. Apparently, they had been very close.

He was showing me lots of trees that needed chopping down, and it turns out that Fiona and her husband have land on Kawau Island covered in trees that need to be cleared. 'Dad would have loved it there,' said Fiona. 'My husband loves his chainsaw, and they used to encourage each other.'

Next, he gave his other daughter, Lisa, some fatherly advice. 'It's important for you to be happy, but you are looking in the wrong place,' he told her. 'You have strived to find happiness in certain places, but you keep getting rejected. Doing the same thing and expecting a different result isn't going to work. To be happy you have to love yourself, and that is not being selfish.' He reassured her that she was going to be successful, but she had to be patient.

Peter was delighted to tell everyone that he was feeling great. He no longer needed glasses, his hair was back, and the shakes in his arm had gone. (Apparently, he hadn't been able to use his arm because he'd had a stroke.)

Peter then brought through a couple of other people, and stepped aside so I could talk to them. One was Carolyn's dad, Jack. He stayed in the background. The other was Carolyn's mum, and she had plenty to say. Peter let his mother-in-law go for it.

'Your mum has realised she made a hell of a mistake in the way she has treated you,' I told Carolyn. 'She was harsh and she was stubborn, and she regrets every second of the way she was towards you.'

Carolyn acknowledged that, thanks to her mother, she had a very tough upbringing and was not shown any love. 'If I ever hurt myself there was no point in telling her, because she would just say

"That's nothing – you won't die". I was scared of being strapped if I complained.'

I could tell that her mum was the sort of person I wouldn't have had an issue with if I had met her; she came across as quite normal. But it was a different story with her daughter.

'That's absolutely correct,' said Carolyn. 'She made out that she was a kind person and she could be to other people, but she was really hard on me.'

Her mother was genuinely sorry. 'She wants me to tell you that this is her formal apology and she is so sorry for not being the sort of mum she should have been. You have everything your mother didn't have, so she was envious of you. You have had a good family and a loving husband, and you have a good heart. She knows she was wrong.'

Carolyn was in tears as she said, 'I needed to hear that. Now I can finally forgive her, which I haven't been able to do before. I can forget the hurt and I can move on.'

I was so happy to hear that. I knew that it had been really important for Carolyn to get an apology from her mum, and that happened because her husband Peter had paved the way for her to come through. He must have known how much his wife needed to hear the words 'I'm sorry' from her mum.

The atmosphere relaxed a little when Peter came back. He was so pleased to have had the chance to tell his wife and his family that he was okay. In fact, he'd been trying to do that ever since he passed in 2013.

Carolyn had ordered a heart-shaped wreath of red roses for his funeral, and since then the family constantly see images of hearts everywhere. And not just actual hearts, but patterns in places where you'd least expect to see them. They frequently see things like heart-shaped patches of oil on the ground or heart-shaped splodges of foam. Carolyn has even noticed that the creases in her bed sheets left an outline on her wrist, and that was in the shape of a heart.

They are signs that he is there with them, and I think that is pretty cool. He is showing his love for them in the best way he can.

Two halves of a whole

Who's not a fan of a love story? Jack and Rose from *Titantic*, Romeo and Juliet, the blue couple in *Avatar* . . . Admit it, we all love to see people finding that special someone, although it's not so great when it ends in tragedy. Still, at least they got to know true love.

Often we look at relationships in books and movies as examples of an all-encompassing love that we should be aspiring to. Then there are the real-life romances that are examples of great passion and devotion, like Queen Victoria and Prince Albert, Anthony and Cleopatra, Helen of Troy and that Paris guy.

The thing is, while it is all very well being infatuated with someone who sweeps you off your feet, I think the couples we should be celebrating for their true love are the Ernies and Marjories, the Anns and Keiths, and the Carolyns and Peters of this world.

You probably know couples like them, or maybe you are fortunate enough to be part of one yourself. I'm talking about those folk who have been together for ages and weathered many storms. They've raised families, nursed ailing parents and supported each other through everything from job losses to ill health. Little habits may niggle – the way he hogs the remote control, or her tendency to cover every surface with knick-knacks that gather dust – but in the big scheme of things, these niggles are not important. It's not about grand gestures and expensive tokens of their love, it's the thoughtful things they do for each other, like delivering tea and toast in bed on cold mornings or doing those household chores the other one hates.

The flame of passion may not be burning fiercely anymore, but instead these couples are warmed by their mutual respect, affection and love for each other. They're two halves of a whole, and when one of them leaves this world the other is left with a gaping hole in their heart that won't be filled until they meet up on the other side.

It really is a joy for me to feel the depth of this kind of love and to be able to reunite these couples, even if it's just for a few beautiful minutes at one of my shows.

CHAPTER 20

You've got a friend

Around eight times out of 10, the readings I do involve connecting spirit with a family member or partner. But every now and then spirit comes through for someone in the audience who is not related to them. They may be a childhood friend, a best mate, a long-time colleague or even a neighbour. The person getting the reading may be surprised as they thought their mum or grandad would be ahead of this person in the queue, but I get what I get, and they've come through for a reason.

Normally I can tell exactly who I am meant to be reading for, or at least I have a good idea about the general vicinity they are in and it is a quick process of elimination to find them. It helps when spirit stand behind them and tap them on the shoulder.

But in one North Island show I had a shy spirit who was hiding behind the curtain and not showing me who she was there for.

'This girl is about 19 or 20 and she was on life-support, or something similar,' I said. 'Does anyone know who this could be? Maybe a sister or a cousin?'

It took a little while, but eventually a woman put her hand up and said the person coming through could be someone she had looked after for seven years as a caregiver.

'She's really shy, she doesn't want to come out from behind the curtain – that could be something to do with the way she looked in life,' I said. 'Was she on life-support?'

The woman in the audience, whose name was Liz, said no. But I was seeing this girl in spirit hooked up to a machine, with wires everywhere.

'Why does she look like she was wired for sound?' I asked.

'She was on dialysis,' Liz explained.

The girl still wouldn't come out from behind the curtain, but I was getting the most unbelievable feeling of love for Liz from her, even though there was no family link. 'This unconditional love is so pure, you are never going to experience this kind of thing again in your life,' I told Liz.

This girl was really funny. 'She laughs and dribbles at the same time,' I said. 'I don't mean that in a negative sense, that's just the way she was.'

This girl, who I later found out was known as Tee, wanted me to tell Liz that her body was wonderful now. 'She is happy to tell you that there is no more pain. She is whole again.'

Tee told me that as well as needing dialysis, there had been other things wrong when she was on this side of life. She was talking to me clearly, and she had a hilarious and unusual laugh.

As well as seeing that she was no longer disabled, I also spotted feathers – she had her wings.

'Now she's on the other side, she's an angel,' I told Liz. 'But in fact she was an Earth angel when she was here: she taught people to love. Not everyone thought that she was an angel because they were too arrogant. She is saying they had – I can't swear, can I? Okay, she is saying they had their heads up their . . . in the sand.'

That made everyone laugh, including Liz. Meanwhile I could see that Tee was smiling from ear to ear, because she was so happy to be communicating with this very special woman who had been an important part of her short life. She was quite forthright, this young girl, and I really liked her.

'You could tidy your room,' she told Liz. 'Get rid of some of the crap you don't need, especially under the bed. You are not a messy person, but things have got away from you because you are so busy.'

She also pointed out that Liz was not the best driver in the world, because she got stressed behind the wheel. 'Just take it easy, but know that she is there watching you. She's your angel now, just like you were hers when she was here.'

Tee thought Liz needed to get on a plane and go somewhere nice on holiday, maybe Australia or the islands. 'It's something she really thinks you should do, and not only for yourself. Where you go, she goes – and she wants to go on holiday!'

I could see a couple of kids on the scene, and it turned out one was Liz's child and she looked after the other one. Tee was telling Liz through me: 'I promise you that I will look after the kids. You fear losing your child and the other one. This has got to stop: you are not accepting life; you are fearing life and that makes it harder. Stop worrying about things that haven't happened – I will take care of the kids.'

Things were starting to wind up and Tee was ready to go. But there was something else she needed to tell Liz, and it was really nuts.

'I've got the goldfish with me,' she said. 'Don't worry about it.'

Liz laughed at that.

'It just died last week,' she told me.

That made everyone chuckle, which was what Tee wanted.

'You always made her smile, and she couldn't have done it here without you,' I told Liz. 'Don't forget to make yourself smile. Book a holiday, have some fun. You deserve it. You are an amazing human being and you give so much to so many people. She wants to thank you for everything you did for her.'

As far as my readings go, that one was pretty short and sweet, but Tee was able to say exactly what she wanted to Liz, and I got the feeling it was all stuff Liz needed to hear.

In cases like that, I love being the messenger boy!

Liz says

I'm a social worker, and I looked after Tee for seven years as she was in the foster-care system. She had spina bifida and was in a wheelchair, and she also had an intellectual disability and kidney failure. She'd had a transplant, but it didn't work, so she was left with no kidneys and had to have dialysis for four hours every second day. But she would only do an hour at a time because of the pain, and in the end she just gave up. She died aged 19.

I would fight for her and advocate for her. When she passed away I had to organise her funeral. The theme was butterflies – the saying 'Fly high, my butterfly' was her thing, and there are butterflies on her grave. She wanted to be a butterfly and now she has got her wings.

Her laugh was amazing, like Kelvin said, and she also had a mouth on her. It was interesting that he said she hung around behind the curtain, because she spent a lot of her life behind a hospital curtain. She would spend weeks in hospital with lots of complications. I was the one who would be telling the doctors to listen to her.

It is so good to hear that she is free of pain, because she suffered so much. Some people thought she was being naughty, instead of understanding that she was in pain. When Kelvin said what he did about people having their heads in a certain place, that was so accurate. That was what she had to deal with every day. People didn't always listen to her. I would go in and tell them what she was going through.

Tee was special. I have looked after people with disabilities for over 20 years, but she is the only one who touched my heart in that way. You usually have to put boundaries up, but with her there were no boundaries.

It made me laugh when Kelvin talked about the messy house. My house is a mess at the moment because I am so busy. I don't have a holiday planned, but I think about it every day! Now I will have to go somewhere.

I do worry about losing the kids I look after because of their medical and disability issues, and after what I went through with the trauma of losing Tee I worry about my own child as well.

And as for the goldfish . . . I look after Tee's flatmate, and when I went to see her yesterday she said the goldfish had just died. For Kelvin to know about that was the icing on the cake.

It felt amazing to hear what Kelvin said. I feel lucky to have had that message and to know Tee is free of pain. She was beautiful and I miss her so much.

Besties reunited

Have I mentioned how much I love the way that spirit work? One of the things they often do is bring in other spirit who need to connect with someone in the audience. That's really unselfish of them. Instead of hogging me and having as much time as they can chatting to their loved one, they will often hand over to another person who needs to come through.

That happened in Christchurch, when I was reading for a mum called Gayle and her daughter Kara. When I counted spirit around them, there were nine people. I couldn't read them all, so I had to work out who I needed to speak to first.

Gayle's dad was there and so was her mum, and after a brief chat with Dad, I established a good connection with Mum, who was a real sweetheart. She let me know how happy she was to be back with her husband, the love of her life, and I could tell they were a beautiful couple. There was a serious message for Gayle's husband about sorting out his health, and a thank-you to Gayle and her sister for looking after Mum when she was sick.

Then Mum said the name Catherine, and indicated that there was a person there in spirit who had something to do with her granddaughter Kara.

'That's my best friend, Cathy,' said Kara. Her gran went and got Cathy and brought her closer to me. As soon as Cathy realised where she was and that I could see her, she went, 'Hi! Woo-hoo!' She was so excited to be there and more than happy to be in the spotlight.

'She's quite flamboyant, your friend,' I told Kara. 'She's very bubbly and outgoing.' Kara was nodding her head in agreement. 'She's still the same person over there that she was here,' I said. 'She's so thrilled to be here and she really wanted to see you, but she waited graciously in the back for your whānau to come through first, and now thanks to your gran it is her turn.'

I couldn't get over how much fun Cathy was – the life and soul of the party. She was a real chatterbox, and she was showing me that she liked to do silly stuff. I could see her on a pair of those old-fashioned four-wheeled roller-skates you strap on, and making mix-tapes with music cassettes.

She was looking at old photos, and telling Kara to make sure they were looked after in plastic folders. Although she added, 'Some of them you can throw away!' Kara laughed at that.

Cathy said she was so sad she didn't get a chance to say goodbye, but added that she was with Kara a lot.

'When you are stuck in traffic and you get stressed and start hurling abuse out the window, she is sitting in the back seat laughing her head off at you. By the way, she says she doesn't mind your music – most of the time.'

On a more solemn note, she told her mate that she was watching over her children. 'You tend to have a big fear about them leaving before you, but don't worry about that because it isn't going to happen.'

Cathy asked Kara to tell her other friends that she was okay. When I asked her what the main message she wanted to share was, she replied, 'Just tell her I miss her and I love her.'

Kara, who was rather tearful by that point, wanted to know if Cathy was all right. 'I am, and I am so happy that you came along and I have been able to talk to you,' Cathy said to Kara via me.

I was delighted to tell Kara that Cathy now has her wings, and is an angel.

It turns out Cathy was only 41 when she had died unexpectedly from a heart attack, six years earlier. She and Kara had met when their kids went to primary school together and had immediately clicked. 'We were inseparable for a bit,' said Kara.

She said that I got Cathy to a T, and she was definitely very outgoing and bubbly – 'an amazing person'. 'I am not surprised that she came through going "Ta da!",' added Kara.

Kara feels Cathy around her all the time, so it was no surprise to hear that she would be yelling at her from the back of the car. She does worry about her children, so it's nice to know Cathy is looking out for them.

She said the fact Cathy, who was a much-loved mum and school teacher, has her angel wings is well-deserved, because she was an angel during her time here on Earth. Kara often sees white butterflies whenever she thinks of her friend.

It was a huge shock when she died, said Kara. 'I probably still haven't got over it, but I know she will be in a good spot and not as stressed as she was before she passed. Thank you so much for letting me know she's okay.'

Kara, you are most welcome.

Phone a friend

It is interesting how many parallels there are between the readings with Cathy and Tee. Both have their angel wings, both like to hitch a ride in the car with their mates, and both of them will be looking out for their friends' children. And butterflies had special meaning in both cases.

For me, it was a pleasure to be able to bring them through to their mates and feel the strong bonds they had. It certainly reinforces for me that the love friends share can be every bit as strong as that between couples and family members. And sometimes it can be stronger.

I've written about the incredible love some people have for their families, but unfortunately there are many others who do not get the love, support and attention they need from their parents, grandparents, siblings and even their kids. Remember Carol and Carolyn's readings, and how their mums came through to apologise for not treating them well? How awful it was for them growing up being constantly criticised and feeling unloved?

Unfortunately, I come across situations like that fairly often at my shows. In among the readings where there is so much love that it feels like I'm wrapped in a blanket of warm, fuzzy feelings, there are those where the atmosphere is prickly and cold, and it's more like cuddling a cactus. Those are the situations where there has been abuse or neglect or perhaps indifference, which can also be hurtful.

It can be so, so hard to come to terms with the fact that you're not loved or liked by a family member. And it can work both ways: try as you might, you may find it hard to love someone you are related to, and who you are meant to love. In a scenario like that, you have to do your best to get on with the person – such as finding common ground – and try to be as civil as possible. You may also want to ask spirit for help. Try saying, 'Hey, Nan, my sister is really driving me nuts and I can't stand being in her company a minute longer. Can you help?' Your nan will do what she can – after all, she loves the two of you. So you may find that the next time you're together at a family gathering you'll start talking about how Nan used to take you both to the playground and have a go on the slide with you, and as you laugh together over the memories, some of that animosity you hold towards each other will slip away and you'll be bonding. It doesn't mean you're best mates, but you're no longer at each other's throats. Just try it and see what happens.

Of course you may find that things don't improve. You may have to come to terms with the fact that the two of you are never going to gel, and accept the situation for what it is. That's okay. Don't beat yourself up. It is what it is. In some cases you are better off without your families, and you need to get that support and love we all require from somewhere else.

And that's where friends are so crucial. Unlike family, who you are kind of lumbered with, you can decide who you are going to be friends with. You can choose to spend time with people you click with, whose company you enjoy.

Really strong friendships can make a huge difference to your life – this is something I am acutely aware of. I am so blessed to have amazing friends. I've already told you about Uncle, and how important he is to me. This cool Māori dude is my best friend, and I would not be here today without him. He knows me, warts and all, and he gets me, and he's there for me. I do the same for him, and that's what friendship is all about.

I have other friends who also make my world a better place. They come from all different backgrounds – farmers, real estate agents, businessmen, psychologists, prison officers, builders, engineers, electricians, fishermen, shop assistants, salespeople – and they live all over the country. Some I see only occasionally; others drop in to my place a couple of times a week, and vice versa. But I know I can count on them, that they have my back, and they know I will do the same for them.

The thing with friendships, though, is that you have to work on building and nurturing them. Don't expect the other person to do all the running. Stay in touch regularly, help out in little ways if you can. Put yourself in their shoes and ask yourself how they must be feeling, especially if they are going through tough times. And set aside time to simply hang out, knock back a coffee or a few beersies and just talk. It's not hard.

The thing is, it really is worth it. Studies have found that being lonely is as bad for your health as smoking 15 cigarettes a day. Lonely people are 50 percent more likely to die prematurely than people who have healthy social relationships. That's troubling, but at least we can do something about it, and do our best to foster our friendships.

I want you to do something for me. I want you to pick up the phone and contact a friend you may not have spoken to in a little while. Don't make a big deal of it, don't tell them, 'I'm ringing you because that spooky guy off TV told me to.' Give them a call, say, 'Hi, I have been thinking of you – what have you been up to?' and see where that goes. A quick call may be enough, or it might lead to you arranging to meet up. Whatever. Just do it for me today (or tomorrow if you're reading this at night – they may not be too pleased if you call after they've gone to bed).

And then next week, do the same thing with another friend. Try this for a few weeks in a row and see how things go. Note how good it makes you feel, even just chinwagging about nothing in particular, and having someone ask you 'Hey, how are things going for you?' This is the power of friendships.

Then, after you've got in touch with a few friends, when you have a couple of minutes of quiet time, I want you to sit down, close your eyes, and think of a friend who is now in spirit. It could be the bestie you lost tragically a little while ago, or the friend who died when you were kids. Or it could be someone you were close to a few years back but hadn't seen for quite a while when you got the sad news that they'd died.

I want you to picture them and let a few memories run through your mind. And then say 'Hey mate, it's me. How are you?' The next thought that pops into your mind will be their response. Have a little conversation in your mind, and see how that makes you feel. Know that they'll be chuffed that you remember them and are taking the time to say hi.

Talking to your friends who have died is not morbid or crazy. It is recognising that the bond we have with people does not break when one of them is no longer on this side of life. And it shows that friendships can be just as strong – and in some cases stronger – than family ties.

CHAPTER 21

Q and A

If you've ever been to one of my shows, you might notice that in between readings I will usually ask the audience if they have any questions, and I will spend a bit of time providing answers. This is partly to separate out the readings, and clear away one lot of spirit before I start on the next, but I also do it because I know that when it comes to how spirit work there's plenty of stuff many people are confused about.

Some people are shy about putting their hands up, or are concerned that their question might sound silly. Please don't feel this way – we all need to learn somehow, and the answer to your question might be relevant to other people in the audience. So please, feel free to ask away!

And in case you can't get along to one of my shows, here are the answers to some queries I've had recently.

Can spirit move physical objects?

Yes, they can. It takes a lot of effort and energy on their behalf, but they can do it. Ever noticed things out of place around your home? Maybe the ornament that is usually carefully placed in position on your sideboard keeps ending up out of alignment, but you haven't touched it. Or a book sitting on your bedside table mysteriously opens to a particular page and it couldn't have been the wind.

Remember, back in Chapter 8, the photos hanging on the wall in Lisa and Karen's house that moved despite being stuck to the wall with putty? This is spirit seeking attention. A lot of people seem to think that when that happens it's something sinister, especially if things in your home break or make noises. But it isn't. You've been watching too many movies about poltergeists if you think that. It's actually a friendly way of spirit saying 'Hey, I'm here'.

If you can't find an obvious explanation for why these things happen, try being relaxed and saying 'Oh, kia ora!' to your loved one. If you acknowledge them, they'll stop doing it.

I told one woman that her late husband was responsible for moving her garden ornaments. It turns out she'd been blaming her son-in-law, and it had absolutely nothing to do with him.

While moving physical objects is really hard for spirit and takes a huge amount of energy, it is easier for them to interfere with electricity. How many people have been at one of my shows when there has been a problem with the sound? It happens time and time again, and it drives me crazy. We always do a sound-check before the show starts to make sure everything is working and that we have the levels right, but on numerous occasions I'll be talking and the headset will completely cut out.

This is spirit's fault. This happens not only in small venues where there are usually very basic sound systems, but also in large theatres where there is top-of-the-range technology and a crew of sound people who are highly skilled in what they do. I've lost count of the number of times the sound guy has said to me afterwards, 'I have no idea why the microphones were playing up.' I do, mate!

At one show, a really poignant reading was disrupted when the sound died. When I glanced up to the sound box, I could see the guy in there looking rather panicked as he tried to work out what had gone wrong. I could also see his dead father standing next to him.

I don't think Dad in spirit was the reason why the sound was playing up – I reckon he was there trying to help his son. I suspected it was more likely to be spirit I was reading for, who had been a bit of a rat-bag on this side of life, so I asked them to stop mucking me around, and fortunately, after a few seconds, we had sound again. This is what spirit can do.

They also like to play with lights. If the lights in your house flicker a lot, it could be dodgy wiring and so it would be a good idea to get an electrician in to check it out. You don't want to mess about with anything electrical. But it could also be Nan or Mum or your hubby letting you know they are there.

Many years ago, when I was still doing private readings, I did one for a woman who said the lights in her house were playing up. In particular, a lamp in the guest bedroom kept switching itself on. Her husband had tried to work out if the switch was faulty, but it seemed to be working all right.

'It's your nan,' I told her. 'She's trying to get your attention. She's saying "Hey, I'm here!".'

'Oh my God,' said the woman. 'The lamp used to belong to my nan.'

'Well, there you go,' I said. 'She's playing with the lights.'

We continued with the reading, and about five minutes later there was a popping sound and the light in my office blew.

'Oh hello, there's Nan again,' I said. She'd figured out how to tutu with electricity and was using that ability to let her granddaughter know she was around.

Doorbells are the other thing spirit love to play with. A woman told me that she was at her wits' end because the doorbell at her home kept ringing and nobody was there. She had even disconnected it so there was no electricity going to it – and it still rang.

'Tell your dad to lay off, that you know he's there and he doesn't have to attract your attention that way,' I advised. Problem solved!

Do you ever read for the wrong person by mistake?

No. But sometimes there can be a few technical issues, so to speak, when getting started. Usually spirit make it pretty clear to me who in the audience they are there for. Either they will tell me – 'My lovely wife is the lady with the curly grey hair and the pink top' – or they will go and stand behind them, and tap them on the shoulder.

If spirit is not being very clear for some reason – maybe they are shy, or they are still trying to get their head around the fact that I can communicate with them, or if it is a big venue and the family member is sat way at the back – it can be tricky for me to figure out who I am meant to be reading for.

On occasion I have started reading for someone only for them to look puzzled and shake their head when I give details. Then I'll say, 'Okay, if it is not you, who is the person who just bought a new car?' and it'll turn out to be somebody a few seats along. Usually these teething problems are rectified pretty easily.

However, the other thing that can happen is that I will get a crossed link. This is what happens when I'm surrounded by so many spirit, all trying to get my attention, that they'll start jumping in on someone else's reading.

I'll be reading for somebody and nailing everything I tell them – 'Your dad used to love working on cars, he played golf and I'm hearing an accent, so he must have been from Europe somewhere' – and then I will mention something that does not resonate, such as 'Did he sing in a choir?' Their dad was tone-deaf, so that makes no sense at all. Nobody else in the family can sing, and in fact they're not fans of music. Then I'll pass on some more information I'm being given and none of this will mean anything either. By now the audience is probably thinking I've lost the plot. But what has often happened is that another spirit has jumped in and I'm now seeing what they're showing me.

Now that I've got many years of experience under my belt, I am a lot better at recognising these situations pretty quickly, and realising I am dealing with a completely different energy. Often you will hear me saying 'Excuse me, can you step aside while I finish talking to this person?', as I'm trying to sort out who I am communicating with. Keeping control of spirit can be like herding cats.

Occasionally a person sitting in the row directly behind the person I am reading will put up their hand and say, 'Actually, I think that's my dad. He used to sing in a choir.'

When I'm reading people at a show, I would rather they tell me if what I am saying means nothing instead of sitting there with a blank expression on their faces, because it could be a crossed link, and if I realise this I can try to get the right information to the right people.

On rare occasions I can find it difficult to work out who spirit is there for, especially if the person I am reading for is touching someone else. This happened at a show where two women were holding hands and I could not work out which of them spirit wanted me to talk to.

Having said this, I read for plenty of people who are holding hands with others without it being an issue. Often, when I start telling someone in the audience that I've got a loved one in spirit with me, the person they came with will grip their hand to give them support. Jo Stirling was holding the hand of her good friend Gina as I passed on information about her missing father-in-law, Curly. That didn't make a difference to the reading – I got Curly loud and clear.

But in the case above, the physical link between the two women made it really hard for me to figure out which spirit was connected to who. And it didn't help that they weren't taking the reading seriously, judging by the way they were giggling.

Someone whose death was due to suicide came through, but they both said they didn't know who that was. That surprised me because there was definitely someone there for one of them who had taken their own life. Other spirit also turned up, including the grandmother of one of the women, so I kept trying to read but it was confusing.

'Do you think you could please stop holding hands, so I can make sure I'm getting the right messages for the right person?' I asked. 'It's really sweet, but because you're touching, it's making it tough.'

They giggled and said 'But we're besties', and continued to hold hands and laugh. In the end I had to give up. I'm sorry to admit that I lost my patience with them because I was so frustrated. It was not only the fact that they were making my job very difficult and disrespecting me, but they were disrespecting spirit, who had made a huge effort to come through. And it was also showing a huge lack of respect to everyone else in the audience who was sitting there hoping they would be lucky enough to hear from their loved ones, and were instead having to witness these two laughing and ignoring everything I said.

I couldn't waste time with them, so I had to cut my losses and move on. I later got a message from someone else who'd been in the audience saying 'You were so rude to those two women'. I'm sorry if that's the way it came across, because it's never my intention to be rude. But being disrespectful is one of the things that really yanks my chain, and I don't have any time for that sort of behaviour.

I do get things wrong sometimes, and I do say things that mean nothing to people at the time but that prove to be accurate once they go home and do a bit of research. The important thing for people to remember when they get readings at one of my shows is to be open to whoever it is who comes through and what they have to say. You can help me read as accurately as possible by answering any questions I have – sometimes I just need to hear your voice to make sure I have a strong connection – and to follow up on any requests, like not holding hands.

That way, we can all leave happy.

Do you ever encounter spirit who don't believe in mediums?

All the time. I have mentioned quite a few examples throughout this book where spirit who have come through to me are gobsmacked to find that I can talk to them. Some have even sworn at me, and sometimes, before I realise it, I have repeated that – like I did with the young guy who died in a car crash and swore his head off when the penny dropped that I could see him.

If people were sceptics on this side of life, it can be a huge shock for them to find out that, actually, talking to dead people is a real thing. And people who were very religious usually struggle at first with the concept of mediums. They've spent their life thinking people like me are evil, and being able to communicate with the dead goes against their beliefs. It can take them some time to get their heads around the fact that, yep, this is really happening.

John Mohi came from a religious background, and when he was alive did not believe in what I do. But he was open to changing his mind, especially when he realised I might be able to help him.

One of the strongest reactions I have had from surprised spirit was at a show in New Plymouth. I was doing a reading for a young lady called Nicole when her dad turned up. He was hanging back, and when I turned to him to say 'Kia ora, bro', he was shocked.

'How the hell can you talk to me?' he said. He was utterly freaking out. He knew he was dead and that he could be around his girl, but he wasn't prepared for the fact that I could put him in touch with her.

I tried to get him to calm the farm by initiating a conversation with him. 'How's your day?' I asked.

'It was okay until I realised you can see me,' he replied. That made everyone laugh.

Eventually I said to him, 'Look, just slow down and take a look at the situation we're in. This is good that I can see you and tell your daughter what you're saying, isn't it?'

That's when it dawned on him that I wasn't just some weirdo – I could help pass on his messages to Nicole. 'I love my daughter, I love her so much,' he said, all emotional. 'I am so sad I had to go.'

Once he understood what was happening, he was able to give me some information. 'Don't give me a hammer,' he joked. It turns out the family had had a hammer engraved on his gravestone.

He also sang 'Happy Birthday' to his girl. 'That's so nice,' Nicole said, 'because most people forgot my birthday this year.'

'Well, your dad didn't,' I told her. 'He misses you and he's proud of you.'

For someone who had been so freaked out to start with, he did a pretty good job of getting across messages that meant something to Nicole. He didn't stay long, and in fact he slipped away without saying goodbye. Many people in spirit say long drawn-out goodbyes to their loved ones as the reading is drawing to a close, and some hang around afterwards because they don't want to leave. But this guy was pretty overwhelmed, and too emotional to make a big deal out of saying goodbye. He wasn't being rude; he was just coping the best he could with a situation that had stunned him.

Does everyone have an aura?

Sure do! And not only do people have auras, but so do animals and even objects. The phone I've just been checking my messages on has an aura, so does the chair I am sitting on. Everything has energy, so therefore has an aura. But the amount of energy given off depends on a variety of factors. For example, a wooden chair, which has been processed from a tree, will give off a lot less energy than an actual living tree.

When it comes to human auras, they reflect what is going on with your energy. Remember the lady Ann, who had only recently lost her husband and had really dark, heavy energy when I read for her? Your grief shows itself in your aura.

If you have a black or dark-grey aura it can indicate you are grieving or depressed, and it can also be a sign of an illness, like cancer, or a drug issue.

A while back I ran into a friend I hadn't seen in ages, and the first thing I noticed about her was her aura. It was really black and kind of fizzy – like someone had shaken a huge bottle of cola and she was standing in the middle of all the fizz. Before she even opened her mouth and said anything, I thought, Uh-oh, she's on P. Unfortunately, I was right.

In contrast, a person who is in a good space will have an aura that is bright and vibrant. In some cases, they seem to glow. You often see amazing auras in pregnant women. You know how people talk about mums-to-be glowing? That's literally what I can see in many cases – this bright light radiating from them. That's because there are two auras coming out of one person. When my son Javan's mum was pregnant with him, it was as if she was one big walking bright light. Her aura was epic.

Some people see auras as a variety of vivid colours. They can work out what is going on with a person thanks to the colour of their aura. For example, a person who has red in their aura might have issues with their reproductive system, or it can also mean that they are angry. If someone approaches me and I can see lots of red in their aura I will brace myself, because I know they are quite fired up about something.

Auras can be a dead giveaway when it comes to what people are really feeling. I've known people who always seem to be happy and cracking jokes, and if you didn't know any better you'd think they are in a good place. Then when you look at their aura, the outer part may be bright and sometimes even flamboyant, but under that there's a layer of grey or black. They're doing a good job of hiding what is really going on with them under the outer stuff.

I've spent time with someone who had an aura like this, and in a quiet moment I said, 'Bro, what is really going on with you?' They were trying to keep feelings of anxiety and depression under control, but it wasn't working. I could see that if they didn't sort things out, the grey layer was going to get bigger and bigger and engulf the rest of it.

Some people are more attuned to seeing auras than others. Then there are those like my friend Aenea, who is a healer, who sense auras, rather than seeing them. They can help her to work out what is wrong with somebody and how to treat them.

If you want to know if seeing auras is something you can do, find someone who doesn't mind you 'experimenting' on them, and sit them down in front of a white wall and look long and hard at them. You can ask spirit for some help, and become aware of going into the 'zone' where your senses are heightened. Don't worry if nothing happens to start with, or if you're seeing only a faint outline around the person. Just relax and go with the flow, and see what happens.

Do animals cross over to the other side?

Oh, yes. It is rare for me to do a show and not be shown pets that are with their owners on the other side. I've seen dogs, cats, budgies, cockatoos, guinea pigs, rabbits, tortoises . . . You name them, they show up over there.

I seem to see a lot of goldfish, which is surprising. I mean, I can understand people forming emotional attachments to dogs and cats and wanting to reunite with them on the other side of life, but goldfish? To each their own, I guess.

Being shown pets is one way of me being able to validate that I have got the right person in spirit. I'll say to someone in the audience 'Your mum has got a yappy little dog with her, and it's running around in circles barking its head off', and that might be the detail that really convinces them. They'll say, 'Hey, that *must* be my mother – she's with her annoying fox terrier.'

Or else it is comforting for them to know that a much-loved pet is now being cared for by a beloved grandparent.

A young lady I was reading for at a North Island venue was beyond excited when her grandfather came through for her. After giving her a lecture about getting rid of the clutter in her house, he wanted me to tell her that he had with him the cats she had owned when she was younger.

'He's not a cat person and he's grumbling about the cats being everywhere, but he wants you to know that they are here,' I told her.

'But there must also be dogs in the family, because I can hear woof, woof, woof! Did you have to get a dog put down?'

'Actually, Mum ran them over,' she said, not seeming too traumatised at all. 'It was when I was a teenager: she ran Scruffy over, then she ran Rosie over the next year.'

Oh dear.

'Well, they're okay, they're with Pop,' I said. 'I thought they were put down, but it seems they were squashed down by your mum.'

As I hastily added, 'Oh sorry, that's not funny', it was too late: the crowd was laughing. It was a bit gruesome, but it lightened the atmosphere.

'You need to tell your mum he's taking care of the dogs and they're okay. She might need to hear that.'

I can't speak dog, so I didn't get Scruffy and Rosie's version of what had happened. I can imagine they weren't too pleased with her mother, but at least they were with Pop, and he seemed to like them better than 'all these bloody cats'.

Sometimes so many animals come through for people that I feel like I'm standing in the kennels or a cattery – they're everywhere. But it can give people a lot of comfort, knowing pets end up with us. And I know that when I make it to the other side, I will be very happy to be joined by my gorgeous dog Pixie.

CHAPTER 22

FAQ on KC

I have explained a few things about how spirit work, so now may be a good time to explain how I tick. Here are a few questions that I seem to get asked quite a lot by audiences at my shows and people I meet afterwards.

Do you like being a celebrity?

Firstly, I don't think of myself as a celebrity, and I find it hard to get my head around the idea of being kind of famous, even after all these years. I see myself as a guy who has ended up with a public profile because the work I do just happened to land me on TV. I know there are plenty of other people doing what I do who aren't well known, but I accept that this is my path, and to reach and to help as many people as possible I have had to become a public figure of sorts.

It's not something I wished for, and as I am naturally quite an introverted person it hasn't come easily. There have been plenty of times when I've wished I could be incognito when I am out in public. This has usually been when I have had my kids with me, and people have been so eager to get to me that they have literally pushed Javan and Jade out of the way.

It's also tough when people spot me when I'm out and about and expect me to read for them. I'll get: 'Hey, *Sensing Murder* guy – is my mum with me?'

They don't always get that this is my personal time and I am off the clock. It's like running into your mechanic at the supermarket and saying, 'Can you pop out to the car park and have a look at my ute? It's making strange noises.' You wouldn't do that.

There have also been plenty of times when being known makes people think they can say whatever they like about me, even if it is not true. Things have been written about me in the media that are a long way from the truth. And don't get me started about what has been said on social media. Some people think because someone has a public profile it's okay to share their opinion on that person, no matter how mean or warped that opinion might be. They forget that famous people are only human. I only get a tiny percentage of what real celebrities cop, and even that makes me wonder how they deal with everything that is said about them.

So yes, there are negatives. But having a public profile can also be a positive thing. It has opened doors for me and led to further work opportunities here and overseas. It means I get greater support for the fundraising I have done, like Movember, because more people know who I am. And it means that on those rare occasions when I feel like I have to pass on some unsolicited information from spirit to a complete stranger – like the guy I did the roadside reading for – they are more likely to pay attention to what I have to say. If I wasn't well known and started saying 'Hey I can see dead people and your mum's here', then I might not get the same respectful response. In some cases, I could even get a fist to the face.

I have met many incredible people through my work; including many I would never have crossed paths with otherwise. I feel lucky to have done that.

Becoming well known does take a bit of getting used to, and there are times when I would prefer to not be that guy off the TV. But I accept that public recognition is part and parcel of the job, and that when someone gains a public profile because of what they do – whether it is as a TV presenter or a sportsperson or talking to dead people – it comes with a responsibility to acknowledge the support you get from the public. It doesn't hurt to be polite, to stop and say hello, to sign autographs (does anyone do that anymore?) or to pose for selfies. And I have thought that long before I ever became well known, thanks to an encounter I had as a child.

When I was about 12 or 13 I was on holiday with some of my friends when I spotted a couple of very famous Kiwi sportsmen. These guys were champions in the sport I was involved with at the time, and they were my idols. I was completely starstruck.

Usually the first thing you did back in those days when you saw someone famous was run to get a pen and a piece of paper to get their autograph. But it didn't occur to me to do that, all I wanted to do was to say hello and tell them how amazing I thought they were.

So we approached them, and I recall that I was excited, but polite. One of them said to me 'G'day, mate'. I asked him how he was, we exchanged a few words and I was on cloud nine. My hero was talking to me, and he was such a nice guy.

Then I turned to the other one to simply say hello, and I couldn't have got a more different reaction. He started nutting off at me! 'I'm sick of kids coming up to me,' he said. 'I've had a gutsful – piss off!'

His team-mate immediately said to him, 'Knock it off, man. Let's go,' and pushed him away. He said to us, 'Sorry about this, boys', while we stood there with our mouths open in shock. He obviously knew that what his friend had just done was not cool.

Maybe the second guy was having a bad day, maybe somebody had just been rude to him. Maybe there was a really good reason why he flipped his lid like that. But being on the receiving end of that response absolutely destroyed me, especially as all I had wanted to do was say 'You're amazing, I want to be like you'.

I was so upset by what happened that I stopped taking part in the sport they excelled at. Having someone I looked up to treating me like that put me right off the sport.

I remember thinking at the time, If I ever become successful and end up being famous, I will never do that. And I remind myself of that on those occasions when I am at the airport trying to haul my luggage off the baggage carousel with my bad back, or in the queue at the supermarket checkout and someone gets in my face. The few words I say to them could have a lasting effect: that sportsman's words and the way they made me feel are still with me all these years later. It doesn't hurt to be nice.

A while back I was out in town running errands and I ran into a friend on the street. We were standing there having a chat when a woman walked past with a couple of kids in tow, looked at me and went 'Oh my God, it's you'. She then started going on about how overwhelmed and starstruck she was to see me, and totally interrupted our conversation. I could have done what was done to me all those years ago and nutted off. But what would be the point of that? She wasn't being intentionally rude, and the last thing I want is to leave someone feeling crushed like I had been. So I just said, 'Kia ora. How's your day going?', we had a little chat and then off she went. Not hard.

When I look back at that incident with my sporting hero all those years ago, and I recall how devastated I was, I wonder whether maybe it happened for a reason. I certainly learned a valuable lesson from it. Back then, never in a million years would I ever have imagined that I would be on TV and people would know who I was. But it stuck in my mind that if ever I was famous, I would never treat people like that. It's just not on.

Does having information from spirit give you an advantage in life?

It has given me a career as a professional medium, so that is definitely an advantage. But if you mean does it help me in day-to-day life because I have insider knowledge, so to speak, then the answer to that is no . . . and sometimes yes.

Spirit tell me what I need to know. Obviously, they don't think I need to know the winning Lotto numbers, because they've never given me those. And they don't tell me when I need to avoid particular romantic relationships, because I haven't had a huge deal of success in that area of my life. Say no more.

But when it comes to some things, I do get insights. Certain people will turn up in my life – US TV director Lisa Statman, for example – and I will know I am meant to be working with them or involved in some way. Or they will tell me 'Nah, don't do it'. That's what happened when *Sensing Murder* was resurrected after years off-air and I was asked by the new production team to work on it. I did only one episode because spirit were telling me: 'No, you are not meant to be here.'

I will know mundane things – like the fact my daughter has helped herself to a packet of biscuits from the pantry and is unlikely to eat her dinner because she's devoured those. Or I might sense that a friend has had a tough day and needs to vent over a beer, and next thing I'll be pulling into their driveway.

The thing is, the fact that I get these insights is not unique to me. We all get them, in the form of intuition – those gut feelings I talked about earlier in the book. But the difference between me and many others is that I recognise them as coming from spirit, and, for the most part, I pay attention to them.

And the other thing I do that is different to a lot of people is that I ask spirit for help. It can be anything from asking my pop whether I should take the boat out fishing that day, through to checking in with my spirit people to see whether I should help out in a murder case that involves some seriously dodgy criminals. I ask, then I see what happens. Sometimes I will hear my pop say, 'No, boy, that problem you've been having with the engine is going to flare up again if you take the boat out today.' Or if I've been asked about a case, I might get a horrible sickening feeling, which I take as meaning 'Don't go there'. I have even had spirit associated with cases I have been asked to help with coming through to me to say, 'No, KC, stay out of it.'

Everyone can ask for help. You may not hear your loved ones in spirit speaking to you, but you could get signs that provide answers to your questions. Just be open to them.

Some of my friends do have a light-hearted go at me for using my 'powers' to unfair advantage. I'm not a big gambler, but every now and then if I'm in a city with some spare time on my hands and a bit of cash, I'll wander into a casino and have a go on the pokies. I somehow seem to know which machines are ready to pay out, and invariably leave with more money in my pocket than I had when I arrived. My mates roll their eyes at that.

I've also been accused of using my ability to communicate with spirit to 'cheat' when it comes to one of my favourite games, Guess the Song, which I wrote about in *Surrounded by Spirit*. I often play it with my team when we are in the car travelling to shows, and it involves trying to be the first person to guess a song and who sings it when it comes on the radio.

I am unbelievably good at this, if I do say so myself, so long as we are tuned into a station that plays classic rock from the 1970s, 1980s and 1990s. I'm no good with the modern stuff, but give me a station that plays The Rolling Stones, Aerosmith, Bruce Springsteen and David Bowie and I will nail it within a few seconds. The reason I am so good is that when I worked as a chef in my twenties we had the radio on in the kitchen all day every day, and I got to know so many songs. It's not spirit whispering 'Elton John! "Rocket Man!"' in my ear, honestly. I just know songs from that genre and era so well.

In fact I am so good at it that a lot of my friends won't play it with me anymore. So a couple of years ago, when I was doing shows in the top of the South Island, I was very happy when a good friend of mine, Kiri, agreed to play, and I'd like to share with you the story of what happened that day.

Kiri – who I call Dame Kiri – is an absolutely beautiful soul, what I call an Earth angel. She's a teacher who does so much for her community – she even spends her own hard-earned money on food so the kids in her class don't go hungry. She's a truly amazing person.

Kiri lives in Nelson and helps out when I do shows in her area, carrying out duties like taking tickets and handing out microphones to members of the audience so I can hear their voices when they get a reading from me. She's a spiritual person herself, and she gets me and how I work. So when I kept getting all the songs right as we drove around in the rental car, she said to me, 'KC, you are so amazing. How do you do this? Spirit must be helping.'

'Nope,' I said. 'Just face it, I'm good.'

One day, when we had quite a long drive between Blenheim and Nelson, Kiri decided, 'Right, we are going to listen to *my* playlist, and see how good you really are.'

She made sure the screen in the centre of the dashboard that tells you what's playing was switched off, so I couldn't see the details, plugged in her phone, chose her playlist, and off we went.

Well, I was on top form. I got song after song right, and not only was I able to tell her the artist as well as the title of the song, but in most cases I was getting the album and even the year it was released correct. I stumbled a few times, but most of the time I was so accurate that she was just blown away.

After two chords of a song I'd be going, '"Changes"! David Bowie! Off the album *Hunky Dory*, released in, ah . . . I think it came out as a single in 1972.'

She'd check what I said and her mouth would drop open.

'How do you know this stuff? You've got to have help; spirit have to be telling you. I don't believe this!'

The more I smashed it, the more she was going out of her skull. She couldn't get over how good I was. By the time the journey was over she was totally bowled over by my abilities, and I'm sure she got out of that car thinking that either I was an absolute genius or I had a direct line to someone in the afterlife who has an encyclopaedic knowledge of rock music. I suspect she thought I had the best-ever spiritual contacts.

The answer – which Kiri hasn't known until she reads this, because I've never told her the truth about what happened that day – is neither. I'm good, but I'm not that good, and nor is spirit.

What Kiri couldn't see from the front passenger seat was that the rental car, a brand-new model, not only had a screen in the centre of the dashboard that showed details of the music playing, it had a second screen by the steering wheel that only the driver could see. Unlike the screen in the middle, that driver's screen hadn't been switched off. So as the music was playing I was reading all the information off the screen.

Because I didn't want to give the game away, I would occasionally throw it every now and then, and say I didn't know what the album was, or get the year of release wrong. There were a couple of times when I had to keep my eyes on the road, so I'd stall and say, 'It's "When I Come Around" by Green Day, the album is *Dookie*, and, uh – hang on a minute, let me think . . .' Then we'd come out of a sharp bend, I'd glance at the screen and say, 'The year was 1995!'

Kiri had absolutely no idea I was doing this, and she's finding out the truth for the first time as she reads this. You don't have to be psychic to know that she'll be calling me all the names under the sun as she reads these last few paragraphs. And I don't need spirit to tell me I'm about to get a phone call from her and she'll let rip. But, knowing Kiri, she will take it as the good fun it was meant to be.

I hope.

How do you cope with all the sad stuff you see and hear?

I'm not going to lie, it's hard. I deal constantly with death and bereavement and people who are very sad – both on this side of life and the other. I can feel their heartbreak, and that often gets to me.

Really tragic cases, like murders, suicides and the death of children, can leave me feeling traumatised. I guess I wouldn't be human if they didn't take a toll on me. I often cry, and when it has come to some really awful murder cases I have actually vomited when the victim has shown me what happened to them.

I cope with the tough stuff in a number of different ways. Over the years I have learned to distance myself a little. I can't take all of the hurt on board; it would cripple me. I also have the assistance of my spirit people, who include my family members and angels. I say my karakia and ask for help in keeping it together while I pass on the messages. I would be of no use at all if I kept losing it big time while trying to read for people.

I try to look for the positives. Yes, it is desperately sad when people lose children, for example, but because I can see that this was their journey, that they weren't meant to be here for a long time, I can instead think that at least the family got to have a few years with this beautiful soul and were able to have the truly special experience of sharing their love. I know a lot of people find it hard to see the loss of a child that way – all they can think is that it is so unfair the child's life was cut short, and look at all the living they have missed out on. Those left behind were cheated out of having that person with them. But if you can accept that this was their path, the pain can be easier to deal with.

When things get really tough for me I have some great people I can talk to, like Uncle, who is wonderful at letting me vent and helping me to understand different situations. He is a very wise man.

Having a busy life as a single dad to my daughter Jade also means I sometimes just have to put the sad stuff away in a box and get on with other things.

Laughter is another great leveller. Yes, there's plenty of grief and tragedy and sadness at my shows, but I try to keep things light-hearted where appropriate, and I love how spirit will often come through with funny stuff that immediately raises people's energy. Some spirit make me laugh because that's the kind of people they were, while others share stories that have everyone in fits.

I had a lovely reading like that when a man called Graham came through for his sister Barbara and their elderly mum, Mavis. One of the first things he said was: 'I shouldn't have had so many Big Macs.' He added, 'When I laughed, everything wobbled.' He said he missed his mum, and he thanked her for cooking him meals and making him cups of tea. Mavis said later that he used to pop around to see her every day, and she'd make sure he had some vegetables.

Graham was a real character. Because his mum was there, I had to word some of what he was saying carefully – if it had just been his sister he would have let rip.

He was a popular dude, one of those guys who would do anything for anyone, but he didn't look after himself. He was so hard-case, he had everyone laughing throughout the reading. He told me Barbara was crap at gardening – she agreed that he was right – and said, in a very funny way, that she needed to learn what a rake was for.

'He would have people on all the time, he was very much a comedian,' she said.

Then I asked Barbara if she was a cat person.

'Nope, not me,' she said.

'So why would he be going "meow, meow, meow"?'

'Oh my God!' said Barbara. She explained that when they were younger there had been a rumour that a local restaurant used to serve up cats and dogs instead of other meats. Graham had wound her up, telling her that she was being investigated by the police and the media for spreading gossip about the restaurant. Not long afterwards she was walking to work one day when he drove up alongside her, wound the window down and yelled 'Meow!' at her, making her jump.

'That's why he'd say "meow" now; it was a joke between us for years. Nobody outside the family would know that, it was our thing.'

The story made the audience laugh, which I think everyone appreciated because there had been a few sad readings.

I said to the audience, 'Folks, you guys didn't know this gentleman, but he's made you smile for a moment and that's the kind of character he was. He liked to make people happy.'

I'm so glad he came through for his sister and his mum – and made the rest of us chuckle.

It's moments like that which help to lift the sadness and make us realise that even if you are dealing with grief and loss, it's okay to laugh and be happy. In fact it is crucial to do that – it will help you to cope, and that's what your loved one wants.

What would you be doing if you weren't a medium?

Good question! The one thing I know I wouldn't be doing is what I used to do: working as a chef. I wouldn't be able to stand all day, given the state my back is in.

I suppose I'd be keen to do something connected with my passions, so pretty much anything to do with fishing. Presenting a TV show on fishing would be a dream come true . . . Oh, hang on a minute, that's what I'm doing!

Other than that, running a business associated with fishing would probably be my cup of tea, whether it is selling all the gear you need or taking clients out fishing.

If we're really thinking outside the box here, one of the things I would love to do is work with cadaver dogs. I got to see what they do up close when I was in the States working on *Voices from the Grave*, and I am in awe of them, and their handlers. What an incredible job they do locating human remains.

You might want to skip this next bit if you're sensitive, but what I have learned is that dead bodies emit a type of gas that can be dispersed through air, water or soil, wherever they have been left. The dogs are trained to pick up on the scent these gases give off. It's the same theory behind how a dog is able to find a bone it buried ages ago. It's not that it has an incredible memory, but because that bone gives off a scent the dog can smell.

These gases, called volatile organic chemical compounds, can travel a very long way from the body – cadaver dogs can find human remains buried up to 4.5 metres deep, and as far as 3 kilometres away. They can also find bones that are hundreds of years old, and they are able to sniff out tissue, blood and other bodily fluids. They are so good that they can even detect residue scents, meaning they can tell whether a body has been in a particular place, even once it has gone. In one study, a group of German-trained dogs had a 95 percent success rate when it came to identifying pieces of carpet a dead body had lain on for 10 minutes. See why I think they are amazing?

I know it sounds grisly, working with an animal that is highly trained to find dead bodies, but imagine their skills combined with mine when it comes to looking for missing people. We would be an amazing team. Spirit could tell me the general area to go to, and the dog could home in on the exact spot.

I have actually looked into ways of bringing a specially trained cadaver dog to New Zealand so we could use it in searches, but this has proved very, very difficult. Part of the problem is that cadaver dogs need ongoing training, and that includes working in set-up situations with dead bodies. In the United States they have these body farms where they strategically place corpses and body parts in a variety of situations, from buried in the ground or kept in water to exposed to the elements. This is partly so scientists can study the decomposition of bodies in a variety of circumstances, which is crucial when it comes to helping to solve crimes. But it is also a way of training cadaver dogs so they can pick up the scent of bodies, including those that have been buried or are underwater. We don't have those kind of establishments here, and you can't just pop down to the morgue and say 'Could you please chop me off an arm so I can bury it and train my dog to find body parts?'

Some other cadaver-dog training aids have been developed. These include bottled versions of putrescine and cadaverine, which are two of the by-products produced by a body as it decomposes. (Imagine having the job of bottling them!) But as these two scents are present in all decaying organic matter, the dog is not getting the full training it needs to find human remains. Pigs can also be used, as their flesh is similar to ours, but humans emit a different scent because of the food we put in our bodies, which is more processed and synthetic. So again, using pig remains is not as good as using actual human remains.

I have done a lot of research into cadaver dogs, and I have found out that a device has been developed that uses odour-sniffing technology to locate buried human remains. It's called LABRADOR, which stands for Lightweight Analyser for Buried Remains And Decomposition Odour Recognition. It is not as good as the dogs – for example, it can only find bodies buried to just over a metre in depth. Still, it is worth bearing in mind that according to the FBI most unofficial graves are shallow, usually around 75 centimetres deep, so this device would still be useful. If I can't work with dogs here in New Zealand, maybe one of these devices would be an alternative. I might have to start saving now!

The thing is, even if I did this kind of work, I would still be using my abilities as a medium to help pinpoint a body. And the truth is that there is never going to be a day when I don't work as a medium. This is my path, what I was put here to do. If I tried to go off and do something else, spirit would kick up an almighty stink.

Remember the movie *Ghost*, and the scene where dead Patrick Swayze hassles the medium played by Whoopi Goldberg because he's desperate for her to help him? Well, that would be me. I would be harangued by spirit until I gave in and went back to working as a medium.

I am always going to be doing this kind of work, although the situations in which I do it might change – for example, I could do more TV and consulting on murder and missing persons cases, and fewer live shows. So maybe working with cadaver dogs will have to be a sideline and fishing will continue to be just a hobby. I'm in this job for the long haul.

CHAPTER 23

And on a final note

Looking back, it's been a pretty epic couple of years. Being me is certainly not boring, that's for sure.

Helping to locate Curly Stirling and John Mohi has been a highlight of not only my career, but my life. I find it so hard to put into words how it makes me feel knowing that I could help them come home to their families. I will be forever thankful to these two men in spirit for coming to me, and to their whānau for trusting me.

Then there has been my work on *Voices from the Grave*. I wish I had been able to go into more detail here about what I've been doing on this US TV show, but, who knows, maybe by the time this book is out the programme will have screened and you'll understand why it has been such a big deal.

Doing the show has been an incredibly intense and mind-blowing experience, and, while it hasn't been easy, it has been a privilege to be involved in this kind of work, and to be part of an amazing team. I am so thankful for the opportunity, and I hope to do even more, because I know that so far we have only scratched the surface of the tragic happenings in LA, and there are a lot more lost souls who need our help.

In the meantime, if you're desperate to see me on TV and have already watched *Sensing Murder* over and over, don't forget you can catch me on my fishing show, *TradeZone Addicted to Fishing*, which I have taken over hosting from Nicky Wilson. This truly is a dream come true for me, and I am excited to be sharing my love of fishing. Now nobody can moan at me for spending so much time on my boat with a fishing rod in my hand. It's my job!

And if you're a sucker for punishment and would also like to hear me, tune into my weekly podcast on www.spreaker.com. Every Monday night I do a live two-hour show, playing music, talking about spiritual stuff and answering questions. Sometimes I have special guests, and if you can't listen when it is going out live, don't panic, the shows are archived so you can listen later. It's a bit of fun, but I also address some quite serious issues, and hopefully people get something out of it.

As I write this, 2019 is drawing to a close and plans are well underway for my final show of this year, another *Pay It Forward* show, with the proceeds going to another cause I strongly support. Sands New Zealand is a non-profit organisation that does a wonderful job of supporting bereaved families who have lost a baby, and Gemma has been working tirelessly to organise this event.

I'm looking forward to hanging out with my Jadey girl over summer, along with my mates. Uncle will be coming to stay, and no doubt we will have some more adventures!

Looking ahead to next year, there's a lot going on. Filming TV shows, the launch of this book, overseas tours . . . I suspect I am going to be pretty busy, but that's okay. That's what I am here for.

I also suspect that there's going to be more mahi (work) for me to do in connection with missing people. I feel really strongly that I need to be focusing my attention in that direction and helping where I can.

When life has to go on

When I phone people to see if I can help them, for example in a missing person case, it can be hard to end the conversation. That's because I'm trying to get as much as I can from spirit while I'm speaking to their loved ones, but also because the family members don't want to hang up and lose the connection, literally. I completely get that.

The call with John Mohi's granddaughter Ronnie was the exception – it was short and sweet. But that was because after eight minutes she had the information she needed, and she had to take it to the search team straight away.

On the whole, phone calls tend to go on for a while, so it was a surprise when a woman I was talking to about her missing brother suddenly cut the call short. 'I'm so sorry,' she said, 'I have to go to work.' I was surprised to hear that, especially as it was about 9 p.m. It turned out she was a long-haul driver and she couldn't take time off. My heart bled for her. She was going through all this trauma because her brother was missing, but she still had to go out and earn a living. I thought of her that night, sitting in the cab of her truck as the kilometres sped past, cut up over the brother who had vanished.

Unfortunately, for the families of missing people, life has to go on. Money has to be earned, bills paid, other family members looked after. You may feel like your world has ground to a halt, but eventually you are going to have to start moving again.

I've done a lot of readings with people in this situation, and I've always wished there was more I could do. I would love to be able to say 'Look, I'll pay your mortgage for the next couple of months while you focus on the search for your brother', or 'Here's some money to cover groceries so you don't have to worry about how you will put food on the table while everything is still so raw and difficult to deal with'. Unfortunately, I am not rolling in money and my bank manager would have a heart attack if I started doing that.

So a dream I have – and may even have got underway by the time this book comes out – is to set up a charity to help out the families of missing people. Obviously we will need to raise quite a lot of money to fund it, but I am confident we can do that, especially when people understand what these families are going through.

In the month Curly Stirling was missing, his son Glenn was out on the Waikato River in his kayak every day looking for his dad. He trawled the water day in and day out, sometimes from dawn to dusk. Daughter-in-law Jo and her friends walked the streets and then clambered through bush hoping to find Curly. Life was put on hold, and it was the same for John Mohi's whānau.

In another missing person case I got involved in a while back, some family members lived overseas, so they dropped everything and took time off work to fly in. Of course they didn't hesitate to do it, but it nevertheless took a financial toll.

In New Zealand we are generally good at rallying around and supporting people going through tough times. We bring casseroles to pop in the freezer, we pick kids up from school, we mow the lawns and do the housework. We're also pretty good at donating to Givealittle pages. I'd like my charity to be an extension of this community support, so we can help to take some of the pressure off. I'd tailor the support to individual needs: maybe they need extra childcare or even therapy to deal with the mental and emotional toll of having a missing loved one. If I can't bring their loved one back home to them – and I know there are some people who aren't meant to be found – then this is the least I can do.

Another dream I have is to be able to provide a place for these families to go to for some quiet time. There are a few stunning remote properties for sale in the Bay of Islands that would be ideal spots to set up accommodation for families to stay for a few days at a time. The locations are breathtaking – private white-sand beaches, rolling hills, tranquil native bush and forests. These places would be perfect for meditation and taking time out from the stresses of daily life. I could spend some time with the families, doing spiritual work and hopefully helping to put them in touch with their loved one.

As well as the families of missing people, I could host those who have lost loved ones in tragic circumstances, like murder. I would love to give families having to live with the pain of grief the chance to experience a bit of calm and peace and to learn techniques like meditation, which can help them when they have to go back to the real world and life feels overwhelming. It would be so cool to be able to show them that they don't need me to communicate with their loved ones – they can do it themselves just by sitting down and having a quiet chat.

When I do a reading for the family of someone who is missing or has been murdered, I may not remember exactly what was said but I instantly recall how it felt. It does have an impact on me, and sometimes I will continue to think about particular cases for a long time to come. But anything I feel is nothing compared with what the family is going through, and will have to learn to live with, possibly for the rest of their lives. That's why I am determined to do whatever I can to help.

Consultant Cruickshank

I would also love to add the description 'police consultant' to the long list of things I do. Another of my dreams is that one day the police will recognise the part that mediums can play in searching for someone who has vanished, and they'll have me on speed-dial for when a case arises.

Imagine, just imagine, if somebody was reported missing and one of the first things the police did was pick up the phone to me and say, 'Hey, KC, got any ideas about this case?'

Imagine if I was able to connect straight away with spirit, and hand over the information I get. You never know, one time I might get details from spirit associated with the missing person that could lead to them being found alive and well. Being able to help the police get to someone who might otherwise be at risk of losing their life would be the ultimate achievement. I honestly believe it could be possible to save lives.

Even if there were a few officers who got in touch saying 'Look, we can't give you credit for it, but we welcome any input you can give us', I would jump at that. I don't need credit and praise, although it's nice to hear when I do get it. What I do need is for police to say: 'Hey, can you come and have a look at this case?' I would down tools and drive to the other end of the country in a heartbeat if a team of detectives asked me to join them.

Why do I love doing this so much? This is someone's daughter who is missing, someone's son, or their mother or father. Their families not only have to live without them, but they have to live without knowing where they are or what happened to them.

As I said earlier, there are over 350 families in this country who are in this position. There's so much pain, and so few answers. But I really think it doesn't have to be that way.

AND ON A FINAL NOTE

A show of gratitude

One of the best parts of my job is getting so much wonderful feedback. From people contacting me via Facebook to say 'Thanks, bro', to being swamped with hugs from people I have read for at a show, I get thanked a lot, and I love it.

I know a lot of people do jobs where they barely get a word of thanks from their bosses or the people they deal with in the course of their work. In some jobs, they hardly ever hear anything positive – they get told when they do something wrong, not when they do something good.

Please, please take a moment to thank somebody in your life for what they do. It could be your partner, your parents or your kids, or maybe someone you work with. If you're a boss, let your employees know what they are doing well, even if there's other stuff they're not so hot on. Tell your colleagues you appreciate their efforts.

Show your gratitude to strangers for what they do, including things that are part of their job. Let your kid's teacher know how much they love the energy she puts into storytelling. Tell your hairdresser how much you look forward to the gentle way they massage your scalp when they're washing your hair. A few thoughtful words of gratitude will not only give them a boost, it will help you to appreciate the good things in your life, which is great for your soul.

I'm so blessed to have had a lot of special thank-yous. At my second *Closer to Nature* show, I got chatting with a lady and two girls during a break and posed for a selfie with them. Later, at the very end of the show, the woman, whose name was Denise, spoke out and thanked me for what I do. I then started reading for her, and was shown that her boy was in spirit, there was a connection with Australia, and I was hearing the word 'twin'. It turned out that her son Luke had died and his twin Josh had moved to Australia.

Then she told me: 'Luke's in your book, *Surrounded by Spirit*.'

For a moment I had a complete blank – a lot of stories went into that book. But then it came back to me, how a couple of years earlier I had done an extremely emotional reading with Denise and her partner Stuart, whose boy Luke had committed suicide. He was such a nice kid. He was very good-looking, played rugby and rode bikes, and got on well with people. There had been lots of unanswered questions about his death, and what had driven him to take his life at just 15. But I was able to say to his parents, 'It was nothing to do with you, it was not your fault. He didn't mean to let you down, and he's upset by how upset you are.' Luke wanted his dad to let go of his anger, and his mum to let go of her sadness.

'He's loved over there, and he's safe,' I had told Denise and Stuart. 'And he's very happy that he doesn't have to make his bed!'

He was also able to tell them that he no longer looked the way he had when he died. And then came the best news of all – Luke had his angel wings.

Denise said the reading from me that night had changed her life, and I was very pleased to hear that.

Denise says

I went along to Kelvin's show that night not expecting to get a reading. I believe in what Kelvin does, but I wasn't sure my partner did. Then what he said just rang so true. It had to have come from Luke.

We were both so stressed and angry at that stage, and I had a lot of guilt. I was his mum, I should have been able to save him. Having Kelvin validate how we felt helped so much, and hearing this didn't happen because of us gave us so much comfort. It was also so good to hear that he was okay. I had been so worried that he was still somehow in pain.

The thing that really blows you away when you are getting a reading from Kelvin is that you know your son is really there. He's not gone; he's actually with Kelvin, talking to him and showing him things. That really got to me.

I talk to Luke all the time. I say goodnight to him every night, and I tell him I love him. If I see something that reminds me of him, I say, 'I know that was you, son.' It makes me feel so much better.

I trust Kelvin completely. I know there are people who think, Oh he makes it up, but I know he doesn't. I know he can do what he does because he did it for us. We are a true story.

We miss Luke so, so much, and we always will. But thanks to Kelvin, knowing that Luke is okay has brought us peace and it has helped us to keep going. After the reading with him, I could breathe again.

A thank-you from me

It is so lovely that I could help Denise and her family, and that hearing from Luke made such a difference to them. I wish I could do this for every single person who needs to hear from someone they have lost. Who needs to hear the words 'I love you' and 'I'm okay'.

I'd like to say my own thanks to everyone who comes to my shows, who listens to my podcasts, who interacts on the Facebook page, and who buys the books. Thanks for supporting me, thanks for respecting me, and thanks for trusting what I do.

I plan on doing it for a very long time to come! Ka kite, anō!

Also by Kelvin Cruickshank

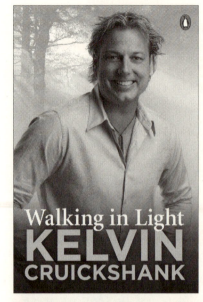
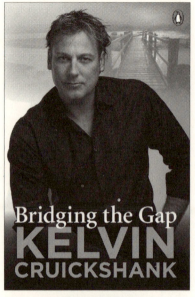
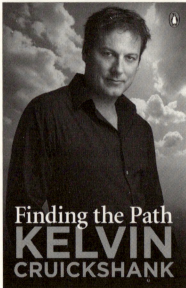
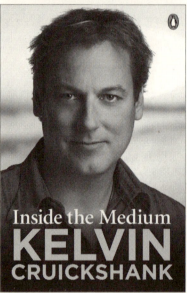

Also available as eBooks

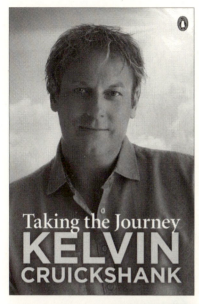
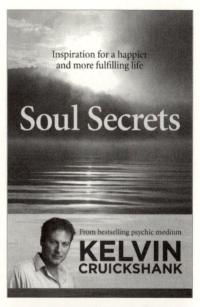
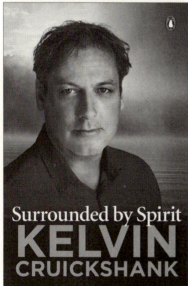
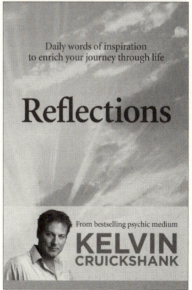

Also available as eBooks

For more information about our titles
visit www.penguin.co.nz